THE

Basic · Basics ·

❊ HOME ❊
FREEZING

H A N D B O O K

CAROL BOWEN

GRUB STREET • LONDON

Published by Grub Street, 4 Rainham Close
London SW11 6SS

Copyright © 1997 Grub Street, London
Text copyright © 1997 Carol Bowen
Jacket design © Nick Denchfield
Design Copyright © 1996 Grub Street
Illustrations: Andrea Darlow

Reprinted 2002, 2004, 2007

British Library of Cataloguing in Publication Data

Bowen, Carol
The basic basics home freezing handbook
1. Home freezers 2. Frozen food 3. Food – Preservation
I. Title
641.4'5

ISBN 978-1-898697-62-6

Printed and bound in Great Britain by MPG Books Ltd,
Bodmin, Cornwall

ACKNOWLEDGEMENTS

I would like to express my thanks to the following companies who have
helped with freezing information for this book:
Birds Eye Foods
British Meat Information Service
Danish Agriculture Producers
Flour Advisory Bureau
Lakeland Limited (formerly Lakeland Plastics)
Long Ashton Research Station
Milk Marketing Board
New Zealand Lamb Information Bureau
White Fish Authority

CONTENTS

FOREWORD

I have been a devoted and enthusiastic freezer owner for so many years that it is easy to forget the days before it arrived. I take for granted a fresh strawberry mousse on Christmas Day, garden-picked peas in November and a fresh slice of my mother's apple pie when she lives some 200 miles away!

For indeed the freezer has liberated our lives. A quick canvass of friends impressed upon me the differing reasons why we have welcomed the freezer into our culinary lives. Reasons like: we can now buy and store commercially frozen foods in bulk; buy foods for out of season eating; shop when we have the time and when we feel like it; shop when the stores are quiet; shop when it's easy to park the car; cook when we feel like it and have the time; cook ahead in preparation for guests or holiday eating; know there is food to hand in emergencies; store good 'cooks' foods or those from a specialist supplier; have no wastage of leftovers; freeze food from the garden that only costs the price of the seed and your labour; buy foods when they are in season and therefore at their best and cheapest; use fuel efficiently by bulk cooking; cope with special diets or illness; and if you hate cooking, cook less often.

Your reason for buying a freezer may concentrate on one particular area in the above list, but all the advantages and benefits mentioned are available to you as you will. However, in order to make the most of your freezer, information on selecting produce, how best to prepare it, how to freeze it and for how long can prove invaluable. This information, along with some basics on home freezing, follow in a simple A to Z format for easy reference. Together with some suggestions for using such foods, I hope you will have everything you need to ensure your freezing efforts are successful.

Carol Bowen

FREEZER BASICS

HOW A FREEZER WORKS

I could seemingly blind you with science here and talk a great deal about compressors, condensers and evaporators but suffice to say, if you want an easy explanation, a freezer works on a simple principle – the extraction of heat from the cabinet. The crucial parts are the ones I have already mentioned and the magic ingredient is the refrigerant vapour. For those of you more technically minded here goes:

When the freezer motor is started, refrigerant vapour is drawn from the evaporator by the compressor and is forced under pressure into the condenser. Here the heat absorbed in the evaporator, together with that generated in the compressor, is given off, and as the vapour cools it condenses into a liquid. The liquid refrigerant is then forced into the evaporator at high pressure through a fine-bore capillary tube or expansion valve and the sudden fall in pressure as it passes into the evaporator causes the refrigerant to boil fiercely, and to change back to vapour (a process that absorbs heat). This is what freezes the food and keeps it frozen. The vapour then passes on to the compressor so that the whole cycle can begin again.

Freezing is one of the easiest and safest methods of food preservation, and the one that preserves food closest to its original state in terms of flavour, texture and nutritional value. If correctly prepared, packaged, stored and defrosted, frozen food will be indistinguishable from its fresh counterpart.

Freezing works by reducing the temperature of the food to a point at which chemical changes are reduced and micro-organisms become inactive. As soon as the food is defrosted, deterioration will begin again.

CHOOSING A FREEZER

Once you have made the decision to buy a freezer, the type you choose will be determined largely by the services you expect from it, the size of your family, the space you have available for it, the money you want to spend and the range of produce you intend to freeze. The needs, for example, of a family with a kitchen and fruit garden, and an avid interest in cooking, may differ from a family of working adults and children alike with staggered meal times or perhaps a working couple without children.

Whatever your needs it always seems better to think big. I have lost count over the number of times that I have heard friends say that they wish they had gone for the bigger model, wished they had more space to take advantage of a particular bargain and bless the friend who had space to cope with an overflow from my freezer during one very busy entertaining period. The more scientific and mathematical might like to know that as a rough guide you should allow 85-113 litres/3-4 cu ft of space for each member of the family. In other words a 350 litre/12 cu ft model is really the smallest you should consider for a family of four people. Remember that each 28 litres/1 cu ft of freezer space will only store between 9-11 kg/20-25 lb food.

There is a large choice of freezers on the market but basically they fall into three categories.

✳ THE CHEST FREEZER
✳ THE UPRIGHT FREEZER
✳ THE COMBINATION REFRIGERATOR/FREEZER

Always spend time comparing prices in as many shops and discount houses as you can before buying. Remember too that you are also more likely to get reliable after-sales service from large reputable manufacturers.

THE CHEST FREEZER

Recognised by their box-like appearance with hinged top-opening lid, the chest freezer's capacity ranges from about 125 litres/4 cu ft up to 775 litres/25 cu ft. Large models usually have counter-balanced lids which will stay open in any position and thus leave your hands free for searching or packaging.

Some models are fitted with a partition to separate the fast-freeze section from the main storage section. In some models the fast-freeze section is separately refrigerated. Some hanging baskets are usually supplied with the freezer, though more may be purchased separately.

ADVANTAGES

1. Because of its relatively simple construction it is usually cheaper to buy than an upright or combination refrigerator/freezer.

2. It is usually slightly cheaper to run than an upright or combination refrigerator/freezer.

3. As items are stacked on top of each other, it is possible to store more food per litre/cu ft.
4. It is considered better for storing large and irregular pieces of meat and large turkeys since there are no shelves to limit space.

5. It usually requires defrosting only once per year.

6. The lid can be used as a work surface in the kitchen.

DISADVANTAGES

1. It takes up proportionately more room than an upright and combination refrigerator/freezer.

2. It can be difficult to find items unless you have worked out a good system.

3. It is more difficult to manage for small or elderly people.

THE UPRIGHT FREEZER

The upright freezer resembles a refrigerator in appearance and will take up a similar amount of floor space. It has a front-opening door, several shelves, often adjustable and/or pull-out baskets so that the food can be seen and easily removed. Some models have a special fast-freeze shelf, drawer or compartment, while in others any shelf can be used for this operation. Again there are a wide range of sizes ranging from around 57 litres/ 2 cu ft to 566 litres/20 cu ft.

ADVANTAGES

1. Ideal where floor space is limited.

2. Packages are more easily accessible.

3. There is possible work surface on some of the smaller models and some are designed to fit on existing work surfaces if this is more convenient.

4. Sliding baskets are useful on some models and are ideal for those with limited mobility.

5. Many have automatic defrosting.

DISADVANTAGES

1. They are generally more expensive to buy than chest models.

2. They are not always able to take large or awkward-shaped packages on their shelves.

3. There is seemingly less storage space per litre/cu ft than in a chest type.

4. They are slightly more expensive to run than chest types, but not as much as is usually imagined.

THE COMBINATION REFRIGERATOR/FREEZER

Some manufacturers produce 'twin-units', which are two separate front-opening models combining refrigerator and freezer, the refrigerator usually having the same litre/cu ft capacity as the freezer. These may be designed to stand on top of each other or side by side. The upright combination is particularly suitable for limited kitchen space.

The freezer unit has a separate temperature control which can be lowered for fresh and pre-cooked foods, but the freezing capacity is usually fairly small, up to about 198 litres/7 cu ft and capable of storing a maximum of 63 kg/140 lb frozen food.

ADVANTAGES

1. Shelves and food are easily accessible like in the upright freezer.

2. It is better suited to long-term storage of commercially frozen food rather than those who freeze large quantities of home-grown food.

3. It takes up very little floor space.

4. Many have automatic defrosting.

DISADVANTAGES

1. Limited storage space and capacity.

2. It won't easily store large or bulky items.

3. Marginally more expensive to run than a chest freezer of the same size.

4. More expensive to buy than a chest or upright freezer.

SITING A FREEZER

This can be almost anywhere which is well ventilated and not damp. As you do not go to the freezer as often as the refrigerator it could be in a spare room or the garage.

If you intend to freeze a lot of your own produce either from the garden or home-made dishes, it is more convenient if the freezer is in the kitchen. Try not to place it next to the central heating boiler or cooker, or it will have to work that much harder at maintaining its low temperature.

Condensation is often quite noticeable when a freezer is stored outside in a garage or in a not so dry cellar. To maintain low temperature inside the freezer it pushes out warm air which, on hitting cold and sometimes damp atmospheric conditions, turns to moisture vapour and deposits itself on the outer casing of the freezer as dampness. Where this happens, owners should dry off any condensation when noticed so that the dampness does not penetrate into the working parts of the freezer (where they could cause rust).

Generally speaking, a freezer stored in the garage should be treated the same as a car, ie kept dry and wax-polished frequently; keep the freezer on boards or bricks so that the metal surfaces are kept clear of the damp.

INSURANCE

Although the freezer is a reliable appliance, some insurance policies include cover for any loss of food through accidental switching off of the power supply and accidental damage to the freezer itself. Frozen food insurance can be obtained to cover loss of food through breakdowns and accidental failure of the power supply. Breakdown and repair insurance (labour and materials) is also available.

It is sometimes possible to have this insurance included in your house policy but since most of these policies are not specific they do not always include the full range of items that you would get from a specialised freezer insurance broker.

MOVING HOUSE

If the distance isn't too far and removal men are willing and able (it might be very heavy) it may be possible to take the freezer with the food inside. Turn the fast-freeze switch on for 24 hours beforehand to get the contents down to as low a temperature as possible, and, if not packed full with food, stuff with crumpled newspaper so that items will not move about, possibly damaging the interior wall of the freezer. Do not run down stocks if you are moving the freezer in this way, the more food the better, but make sure it can still be lifted. Make sure it is the last item to go on the removal van and therefore first off - establish beforehand where it is to go and don't forget to plug it in as soon as possible. Cakes and vegetables and those items which are already cooked will suffer a particular quality loss and may be ruined by a rise in temperature if there is too much of a delay.

If you can't take your freezer full of food then run down stocks as much as possible and pack the remaining items in insulated boxes for the journey. Your removal firm may even be able to supply these. Pack with a little dry ice if you can. Fast-freeze such food for 24 hours beforehand, pack into insulated containers at the last minute and return to the freezer as soon as possible (when it has reached freezing storage temperature). Use insulated containers or make your own temporary ones using cardboard boxes lined with polystyrene begged from your greengrocer, for storing food for short journey times. Take it with you in the car if you can and unpack into the freezer as soon as possible.

CLEANING AND MAINTENANCE

When you first receive your freezer do take the time to sit down and read the instruction booklet that comes with it. It will tell you all you need to know about the cleaning and care of your own specific freezer.

Initially wash out the interior thoroughly before switching on your new freezer. Wash with a solution of 15 ml/1 tablespoon bicarbonate of soda to 1.2 litres/ 2 pints warm water and wipe completely dry. Plug the freezer in and tape over the switch to prevent it accidentally being turned off. Check with the manufacturer's instructions that the temperature control has been properly set. Leave the freezer on for 12 hours before putting in any food. This will ensure that the correct storage temperature of the freezer has been reached and that the freezer is working properly. Ideally do not fill the freezer  completely in one go but gradually; how much fresh food is put in at one time will depend upon its daily freezing capacity.

General maintenance of the freezer is comparatively simple; it should be professionally serviced once a year, and there should be a daily emergency service available in case of breakdown. Check out what services your retailer offers BEFORE you purchase.

Wipe the exterior of the freezer with a damp cloth and dry well. Use a wax or silicone polish occasionally to protect. If the top is used as a work surface in the kitchen then protect it with wipe-over contact paper. This prevents staining, scratching and general wear and tear to the surface.

DEFROSTING THE FREEZER

Usually this is only necessary once a year for a chest freezer and twice a year for an upright or combination refrigerator/freezer, when the contents are at their lowest. This may well be just before the summer season's fruits and vegetables are ready to be harvested; or before you start to stock up for a big celebration like Christmas.

If the freezer is used a great deal and is in a relatively warm place, frost may accumulate on the inside of the cabinet. It is as well to remove this as it appears, with a plastic spatula or scraper.

For complete defrosting, remove the contents; wrap the slow-thaw items in newspapers or a blanket, and put the quick-thaw items into the refrigerator which has been turned to its lowest setting. Remove as much ice and frost as possible before it has a chance to defrost completely, using a scraper and a special dust pan and brush. Wash with lukewarm water. Dry with a clean cloth and set the freezer to fast freeze to reduce the temperature quickly before returning the food.

Do not use a metal scraper, which may puncture the walls of the cabinet.

It is quite possible to defrost a freezer in 20 minutes and therefore it is not such an outfacing job as it might at first seem!

FREEZER BREAKDOWN:
WHAT TO DO IN AN EMERGENCY!

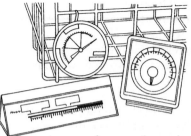

It is the wise cook who invests in a freezer thermometer. For, when placed inside the cabinet, it will accurately record the temperature in the freezer and may prove the very first warning signs that all is not well. Check the temperature occasionally and, if your freezer is in a garage or cellar, then seriously consider fitting a freezer alarm that will give you an audible warning that there is an increase in temperature that needs attention.

Many freezers have a warning light which comes on if there is a temperature rise inside the cabinet. If a temperature above -18°C

11

(the ideal storage temperature) is recorded then check the following before calling your engineer:

1. Are the lights working on the control panel of the freezer? If yes, then move to Point 5, if not:

2. Check that the plug is in and the switch is on. A piece of tape or plaster over the plug and switch is a good idea and label it 'do not switch off'.

3. Has the plug blown a fuse? (This is easily replaced but you should ask yourself why, in case it could happen again.)

4. Look at the mains supply and check that no fuses have gone there.

5. Is there or has there been a power cut? Your mains electric clock is a good guideline as to how long this may have been.

6. Is the lid or door of the freezer firmly shut? Especially with an upright freezer a faulty seal on the door will soon let in warm air. This can be proved if there is a build-up of ice around the door or lid of the freezer.

7. If the weather is hot or you have been 'in and out' of the freezer many times over a short period this may affect the temperature.

8. Has too much warm fresh food been put into the freezer? Even with the fast-freeze switch on, this will increase the temperature of the freezer.

9. Check if there is adequate circulation of air around the freezer and that the grill is not blocked with dirt.

If you have checked all the above points, then call the engineer. Always have the name and phone number of an engineer by the freezer. Remember there is no panic if your freezer does break down, as the contents of a full freezer will be alright for up to 24 hours before the food begins to defrost. The temperature will not normally reach -10°C in this time. Resist the temptation to open the lid or door whilst the freezer is off and also for several hours after it has started working again.

In the event of a freezer breakdown or long power failure, and emergency steps are not taken (if you are away for a few days, for example), the following information will help in your decision on what to do with the food inside your cabinet:

1. If food is beginning to defrost, but there are ice crystals still in the centre of the food, these foods may be refrozen.

2. If there are no ice crystals but the food is still very cold, then bread, baked unfilled products and fruit can be refrozen. Raw meat, poultry and fish should be thoroughly cooked and then refrozen. Remember storage times will then be as for the cooked product. Vegetables should not be refrozen but can be eaten immediately, after being thoroughly cooked. Pre-cooked dishes and ice cream should not be refrozen.

3. If the food isn't even cold then it is not advisable to refreeze any of the food even after cooking, but can usually be eaten immediately after being thoroughly cooked.

WHAT IF THERE IS A POWER CUT?

If the freezer is full the contents will probably remain frozen for almost 24 hours, if only half full then up to 12 hours, providing the freezer has NOT been opened allowing warm air inside. Resist the temptation to look and see if the food is alright.

A power failure will usually have been rectified during this time, but it is perhaps worth putting newspapers and blankets over the cabinet to insulate it if it is thought the failure may be lengthy. It is useful if a friend, not suffering from the same power failure, has room in her freezer, or if you are on amicable terms with your butcher so that you can use his cold room. It is of course possible to insure the contents against such occurrences.

Much more likely than a serious power failure is the chance of switching off the power accidentally. Preferably do not have a switch plug, or, cover the plug with tape and label DO NOT SWITCH OFF! Remember too that you shouldn't switch off the electricity at the mains when you go on holiday! You can have the freezer on a separate circuit.

PACKAGING AND ACCESSORIES

The importance of effective packaging for the freezer cannot be under-estimated, especially if food is to be kept for long periods of time. Packaging ensures that food keeps in perfect condition, protects it from contamination and keeps as much air from it as possible which can cause spoiling also known as freezer-burn. Too much contact with air during freezing can cause dehydration where moisture and natural juices are lost and at its most extreme, as freezer burn, will appear as brown or greyish white patches on the surface of food. Certainly on meat it causes the tissue to go tough and spongy – making it most unappetising. Effective packaging will also reduce or eliminate oxidation (which causes foods to go rancid) and cross-flavouring where some foods would transfer their smell and flavour to others.

❄ Ideally, pack liquids (such as sauces, soups or juices) in rigid containers, but not ordinary glass which could crack, boiling bags, pre-formed foil or polythene packages. Do however leave a headspace to allow for expansion of the liquids when frozen.

Solids plus liquids (such as stews or fruits in syrup) should be packed in rigid containers, pre-formed foil or polythene packages. Again leave a little headspace for expansion and make sure that the solids are immersed in the liquid - crumpled up greaseproof or waxed paper can be placed over the surface to hold them down if necessary.

Solids (like fruits in dry sugar packs) are probably best in rigid containers while most vegetables can be packed in polythene bags. Ready-cooked foods can be packed in the dishes ready for the oven (freezer to oven to tableware is a good investment if you prepare these dishes regularly).

Ideally pack in the quantities you generally use rather than as a mass bulk pack (unless free-flow where you can dip in from time to time, but remember to seal effectively each time).

Packaging materials come in a bewildering array of sizes, colours, materials, prices and durability. Many are one-use throw-away containers and others are designed to last for years. Buy a small selection to begin with and work out which have proved most useful for your own needs before you spend a fortune on a selection that remains unused in a kitchen drawer. Packaging materials can be roughly divided into 3 types: sheet wrapping (such as aluminium foil, polythene wrap, waxed or moisture-vapour-proof paper); bags (to include polythene, boilable plastic, foil and waxed freezer paper); and rigid containers (like waxed, plastic, polythene, toughened glass or ceramic ware and aluminium foil).

All the packaging materials above do a good job one way or another and the choice is often a personal one. Some are however better at storing some foods than others. Make your choice from the A-Z list below:

ALUMINIUM FOIL

Foil has long been recognised as one of the most useful items to have in the kitchen and is especially useful for freezer packaging. It is particularly good for moulding around awkward shapes and, as aluminium is a good conductor of heat, the package will freeze more quickly making it a very satisfactory freezer material. However, make sure that you use catering or freezer foil for freezer storage, as ordinary household foil is not thick enough to withstand low temperature storage, unless of course double wrapped.

Foil dishes: There is a wide selection of foil containers (some with fitted lids) on the market suitable for almost every use. With careful use, foil dishes can be washed and reused several times. The great advantage of this item is that the food can be frozen, defrosted, cooked, and sometimes, served, from the same container. Foil can be attacked by acids in some foods such as citrus fruits, therefore for long term storage do not use for such items.

BLANCHING BASKET

If a considerable quantity of vegetables are frozen regularly it is worth investing in a special blanching basket, otherwise a large sieve or colander will serve the purpose. A particularly good blanching basket is the collapsible one which folds flat for easy storage when not in use.

BOIL IN BAGS

These are made from high density polythene that does not soften above the boiling temperature of water. Foods may be frozen down inside these bags and then reheated by placing straight from the freezer into a pan of boiling water. This is particularly useful for reheating single portions of ready-prepared dishes like curries and casseroles. An effective seal is essential so that water will not enter the bag during reheating and this is done either with a plastic tie, a piece of string or a heat seal. (**NB** As a tight seal is necessary bunch the neck and double over, if string is used tie in a bow knot). The bags, being sterilizable, can be reused. It is also important to make sure that as much air as possible is extracted so that after sealing the food there is enough space for expansion when reheated; if this is not done it is likely to burst under pressure. These bags can also be used in pressure cookers and in the microwave.

CARDBOARD, UNWAXED OR TREATED

Cardboard is a useful protector of delicate food in the freezer. A collar of thin cardboard will protect the sides of a decorated cake, for example. A cardboard base helps to keep a pizza flat and less liable to breakage. It is usual to use cardboard an an additional outer wrapping once the hygienic close wrapping of food has been made.

CARTONS

Cartons made for commercial use for selling such things as margarine, coleslaw, yoghurt etc provide useful freezer packaging, provided they are scrupulously cleaned before use. Some have good fitting lids which can be reused, others have foil lids which will need to be replaced with home-made foil ones. A lot of commercial cartons have not got an airtight lid and freezer tape should be used when necessary.

CLING FILM

This material is made from PVC or polythene and is a thin clinging material. The polythene cling film is slightly cheaper than the PVC but does not have the same effectiveness, therefore most of the cling film sold in the UK is the PVC type. As cling film has so many uses, the large catering rolls are becoming more popular owing to their better value. Most cling film is not thick enough on its own for use in the freezer but can be used double wrapped or as an additional protection, and is ideal for separating small items such as chops, steaks, burgers, fish, cake etc before overwrapping into polythene bags or boxes, so that they can be removed individually.

COOL BAGS OR BOXES

These are insulated bags and boxes available in a wide variety of shapes and sizes. The most useful size seems to be around 20-30 litres/0.75 – 1 cu ft capacity, giving plenty of storage but still an easy size to carry. The best shape seems to be either square or oblong, as this gives more storage for size than a round bag.

Both the bag and the box have their advantages: the bag is collapsible and therefore ideal for shopping trips, the box is better insulated and therefore gives better results. In general terms a good quality cool box will keep food frozen for 10 hours, the cool bag slightly less, assuming that frozen ice packs are used as well.

DEFROST BOX

Ideally, meat and poultry should be defrosted in the refrigerator, but on occasions this is not always possible. For this reason it is now possible to buy a defrost box, which can be used for defrosting meat and poultry etc at room temperature or in the refrigerator. The box has a drip tray to collect juices (that can be used if you like). It has a ventilated cover that protects foods from flies in the summer, and prevents access from hungry dogs and cats! The box also doubles up as a storage container for meat in the refrigerator.

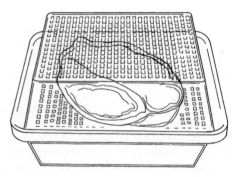

DIVIDERS

These have the same useful purpose as freezer baskets, ie they help with the organisation of food in the freezer into sections so that quick and easy access to the required item is achieved. They are L-shaped and constructed of plastic-coated wire mesh and rest on the base of the freezer. Dividers can be bought in various sizes dependent upon the size of the freezer.

EASY LEAVE

This is high density polythene sheet that can be used as a waterproof tissue in the freezer. It is ideal for interleaving between such foods as beefburgers, chops, sausages, fish, steaks, cakes etc or any portion of food before overwrapping. The layering tissue will ensure that individual food items can be removed without them sticking together, even when still frozen.

FELT TIP PENS

Felt tip pens can now be bought especially for writing on both polythene bags and containers in the freezer.

FREEZER TAPE

This is a tape suitable for freezer packaging – the material is polythene with a special adhesive that remains effective over a long period at low temperatures. This tape can be used for sealing both bags and containers but it can be quite an expensive way of sealing bags. Vinyl tape (rather than cellophane tape) is a cheaper alternative.

GLASS

Not really a very good product for the freezer, as most glass tends to shatter at low temperatures. The exception of course is toughened glass that has been developed to cope with freezer and oven temperatures. Most can be used straight from freezer to oven. Available in a wide range of sizes and shapes they are a good, if sometimes seemingly expensive, investment for general freezer and cooking use.

GREASEPROOF PAPER

This is not suitable for freezer packaging alone since it is neither moisture-proof nor vapour-proof, thus food will dry out during freezer storage. It can however be used with more effective packaging.

MEAT THERMOMETER

This is a very useful kitchen tool for freezer owners in particular, and highly recommended for anybody who likes to cook their meat from frozen (but do follow the guidelines under separate meat entries). Insert the point into the thickest part of the joint, taking care not to touch the bone. The recommended temperatures for different meats, cooked to various preferences, are shown on an easily recognised scale and thus the guesswork of cooking by time is eliminated.

OPEN FREEZE TRAYS

It is possible to buy special rigid plastic trays of a size suitable to fit in the fast freeze section of the freezer. These trays will stack on top of each other when in use so that fruit, vegetables, meat etc can be frozen individually as in commercial freezing. The trays are designed to nest inside each other when not in use therefore saving storage space. However it is possible to devise your own; any rigid plastic tray will serve the purpose, but check that it will fit inside the freezer compartment before you buy.

POLYTHENE BAGS

These should be of the recommended gauge or thickness for use in the freezer (120-150 gauge/30-37 mu) They are available plain or gusseted in a very wide range of sizes. Closure may be with bag ties, a heat sealer or they may be the self-seal type. Coloured bags and mixed colour stripey bags can also be bought for easy identification and location of contents. For example, Lakeland Limited (formerly Lakeland Plastics) sell colour coding bags to help you easily identify the contents during freezer storage (eg red for meat, blue for fish, green for vegetables and yellow for pastries). They come in packs of 100 of mixed colours, size 4 (20 x 30 cm/ 8 x 12 inches) and size 6 (28 x 41 cm/ 11 x 16 inches).

POLYTHENE BAG – HANDY TIPS

* if you need a stronger, less permeable bag for any item and do not have any heavy duty bags amongst your store, one bag inside another of the same gauge will double the strength.

* for items that are irregular in shape or have sharp bones protruding, wrap them in foil or

cling film before putting them in a polythene bag, as this will help to prevent puncturing during freezer storage.

* if you use a colour-coding system, write down the details of your system inside the lid or door of your freezer. It makes finding the required item easier, not only for you but for others, and avoids damage to packaging during rummaging.

* freeze soups or stews in polythene bags using a straight-sided box as a mould. Line the box with the appropriate-size gusseted bag, pour in the cooled food, leaving a 2 cm/¾ inch head-space to allow for expansion, freeze again and you'll have a handy-shaped bag of food and you can use the box again.

* do you want to make crushed ice? Simply put a small quantity into a 25 x 38 cm/10 x 15 inch polythene bag, seal tightly and lay it flat on a tray (an open freeze tray is ideal) so that the water freezes in a thin layer. When solid quickly crush with a rolling pin and empty the crushed ice out of the bag for immediate use, or overwrap in another polythene bag for freezer storage.

* before applying freezer adhesive labels, ensure that bags are clean, dry and grease free. Lay bags on a clean, flat surface and apply label before filling.

* the question often arises about the re-use of polythene bags. Most manufacturers do not recommend this practice, because during freezer storage bags can easily become punctured and also it is very difficult to thoroughly wash bags which have contained fatty food, meat or fish. However, if you feel the bags are in perfect condition, and have only been used for storing items such as pastry, fruit, vegetables etc they can be washed in warm soapy water and given a final rinse in a weak solution of household Milton or similar sterilising agent. Peg the bags upside down on the clothes line to dry.

RECORD BOOK

One should attempt to keep a record book of items both in and out of the freezer to use them in correct rotation and to assess the quantities used and required. I think it is fair to say that those with well organised refrigerators and store cupboards will soon evolve a system of freezer use and identification,

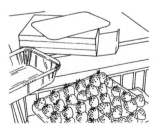

whilst those whose cupboards and drawers are in a permanent state of turmoil (and I include myself here) will find it difficult to be different in using a freezer. No system is dogmatically right, and the one that works for you is the best to follow, whatever books like these and friends try to tell you!

SELF-SEAL BAGS

These bags have an almost 'zip-like' closure operation which enables them to be easily opened and closed frequently. Made of 50 mu/200 gauge polythene in a variety of sizes, they give a good seal. Many also have a panel on the side for easy labelling. Some commercial foods now come in such bags, eg grated cheese for pizzas – consider washing and reusing these bags for freezer storage.

WAXED CARTONS AND BOARD

The coating of wax to card decreases the permeability of the card and makes it an acceptable product for freezer packaging. Such card is available in box, tub, carton and flat card form, some with screw-on lids, others need additional sealing and some fold flat for storage. Although they are reusable, they do stain badly, making it really necessary to line them with polythene, in which case you might as well use a throw-away packet like a sugar or cereal box, lining that to give a good package shape. Unwaxed cartons are unsuitable for freezer use.

FREEZING TECHNIQUES AND TERMS

There are various techniques and terms used in freezer cooking, packaging and storing that may, if you are a novice at freezer usage, seem rather bewildering. What do you mean by fast freeze, open freeze and batch bake?

HERE'S A BASIC KNOW-HOW SECTION TO HELP
YOU THROUGH THE MAZE:

BATCH BAKING OR BATCH COOKING

This is when quantity cooking is done at a 'grand cook-in' session. For example, cook a large quantity of any particular dish and divide into suitable portions for your family; this is especially good for those living alone where cooking small quantities is time consuming, often boring and can prove expensive on fuel. On the other hand it may mean preparing party foods in advance, either complete dishes or components ready for assembly on the day. Yet another example is to prepare a quantity of the same thing for different uses, ie basic pastry or cake mix, stewed steak or minced beef, pie fillings, soups or sauces. Why not consider sharing a bulk cooking/batch baking session with a friend to share the work and the spoils?

BLANCHING

This is the best way of ensuring that the quality of fruit and vegetables to be frozen is maintained over the recommended storage time in the freezer. Not blanching considerably shortens storage life, so any vegetables not blanched should be eaten first. Blanching involves adding the chosen fruit or vegetable to boiling water for the recommended time. The water is then brought back to the boil, within a minute, and the blanching time should begin from that point. Boil for the recommended time then remove the item. Cool quickly in iced water, drain again and then pat dry with absorbent kitchen paper before packaging for the freezer. Blanching water can be used up to 5-6 times.

CAPACITY OF THE FREEZER

This refers to the amount of space available in the freezer for holding food; however, the volume of the food depends on its density and means of packaging, as square shapes will pack more effectively than round packs. Also a shoulder of lamb on the bone takes up twice the space of a boned one. Approximate guidelines are as follows:

30 litres/1 cu ft of meat is approximately 13.5 kg/30 lbs

30 litres/1 cu ft of peas is approximately 11.5 kg/25 lbs

DRIP

This is the loss of natural juices from food, particularly meat. The quicker the freezing, the less 'drip' from the meat on thawing, and unless the resultant drip is used in sauces or gravy, it means that much of the flavour is thrown away and quality and texture impaired. All attempts to reduce drip should therefore be made; some meat is more prone to drip than others; beef and white poultry are the worst sufferers, and pork and dark poultry suffer the least. Drip is least evident when correct ageing, few cut surfaces, low storage temperature and slow thawing conditions are met.

DRY ICE

Dry ice is solid carbon dioxide, which used to be considered one method of keeping down the temperature within the freezer when a breakdown had occurred. Fortunately now, with speedy repair and service teams nationwide it isn't necessary. Dry ice can only be bought from specialist wholesale cold stores.

FAST FREEZING

This is freezing food in the shortest possible time thus preserving its flavour and quality. Your freezer will have a special fast freeze section which is either just an area sectioned off from the main freezer or it may have cooling elements running around all three walls thus improving the efficiency of the compartment. The fast freeze section is the same as the rest of the freezer as regards temperature and can therefore be used for normal storage. For fast freezing put the food as close to the walls as possible to get the lowest temperature, thus freezing the food in the fastest time and getting the best results.

Freezers have a fast freeze switch, usually found at the front of the freezer for easy access, and usually has an indicator light to tell you when it is on. Its purpose is to bring the temperature of the freezer and the food already stored in it down to a sufficiently low temperature -25° to -30°C/-13° to -22°F, that in the presence of fresh food to be frozen, the temperature is never raised above -18°C/0°F. When food is to be frozen, the fast freeze switch should be depressed for several hours (24 hours if possible for a maximum load) before use. The thermostat controlling the temperature inside the cabinet is then by-passed and the compressor works continually until the fast freeze switch is turned off and the freezer is returned to normal setting.

FREE-FLOW

This is a term used when foods, particularly fruit and vegetables, are packed loose in large containers where the amount required can be removed and the pack returned to the freezer. Foods prepared for free-flow use will have been open frozen so that they remain separate and do not stick together during storage.

FREEZER BURN

Freezer burn is recognised by a discoloured dried up surface which in bad cases can be almost powdery when rubbed. It is a form of drying out or dehydration caused by poor packaging and sealing. It does not represent a health hazard but does affect the taste and appearance of the food.

FREEZER LOAD

This usually refers to the amount of fresh food that can be frozen at any one time, ie 10% of total freezer capacity in any 24 hours.

FOR EXAMPLE

IMPERIAL
14 cu ft (allowing 25 lbs per cu ft), 35 lbs of food may be frozen in 24 hours, ie 10% of 14 x 25 = 35 lbs or a medium to small lamb.

METRIC
340 litre freezer (allowing 4 kg per 10 litres), ie 10 litres holds 4 kg of food, then 340 litres is approximately 13.6 kg. 10% of 340 = 34 therefore 3.4 x 4 kg = 13.6 kg.

FREEZING STORAGE TEMPERATURES

Two temperatures are important:

* -25° to -30°C/-13° to -22°F is the low temperature for fast freezing enabling food to be frozen as quickly as possible.

* -18°C/0°F is the normal storage temperature of a freezer at which food is given an adequate storage life.

LABELLING

This is extremely important in the freezer as several products lose their visual identity when frozen and mistakes like tomato sauce instead of raspberry purée can have disastrous consequences!

As much information as possible should be written on the label, including contents, number of portions, date frozen, and if possible best method of defrosting or cooking.

FOR EXAMPLE

DATE
2 portions Minced Beef with Gravy

REHEAT
From Frozen - 25 to 30 minutes 230°C/450°F/Gas 8. If thawed - 15 to 20 minutes in pan.

For vegetables or fruit an indication of variety, and whether blanched or unblanched, in sugar or syrup etc will all prove useful information.

Stick-on labels, which remain adhesive at low temperatures can be bought especially for the freezer. They have a shelf life of about 1 year only. Tie type tags are another useful option since you can label and tie a bag in one operation. The lids of some foil containers also have white card surfaces suitable for writing directly onto the package. It is worth buying extra lids where available if you intend to re-use the containers.

OPEN FREEZING

This is the term most often used to describe the way the home freezer owner obtains free-flow packs like those sold commercially. It is particularly useful when only a small amount is required from a large pack, eg a bowl of strawberries for one, a portion of peas etc.

After preparing the items for freezing, place a single layer on baking trays covered with foil, or wire racks or special open freeze trays, ensuring that the items do not touch each other. Place uncovered in the freezer and

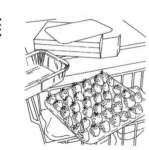

leave until solid, about 2 hours. Then pack immediately into polythene bags or boxes; there is no need to leave a headspace. Don't leave longer than 1-2 hours otherwise dehydration will take place and there is a risk of freezer burn.

Open freezing is also useful for delicate items which could become damaged during packing eg, decorated cakes, piped rosettes of whipped cream or mashed potato.

SEALING

There are a few different ways in which you can seal an item for the freezer:

1. Freezer Tape – this has been specially treated to be adhesive at low temperatures; ordinary cellophane tape is not suitable.

2. Builder's Masking Tape – is also suitable for the freezer.

3. Twist Seals, Plastic or Cellophane Covered Wire Ties – these are the easiest to use for tying polythene bags. Ensure that sharp edges are turned over to prevent perforation of adjacent packages.

4. Rubber Bands are unsuitable since they perish over long term storage.

5. Bag Sealers like those used commercially are available. They seal with a ring of freezer tape at the neck of the bag to a high degree of tightness.

6. Heat Sealers – these have been around but have become increasingly hard to find. They seal, by heat, two pieces of polythene together. The same effect can be obtained by sealing with an electric iron set at its lowest setting, protecting the polythene by two sheets of tissue paper. I have also achieved the same effect with success using curling tongs!

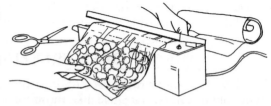

SYRUP PACKS

This method of freezing fruit is generally chosen for those that discolour quickly and those which have very little natural juice. The strength of the syrup used is determined by the sourness of the fruit and personal preference. Medium strength is suitable for most tastes and fruits, but a lighter one should be used for delicate fruits. The amount of syrup to fruit is about 300 ml/½ pint to 450 g/1 lb and sufficient syrup to cover the fruit in the packaging should always be used, or discolouration will take place.

Either put the fruit straight into the bowl of syrup and then portion and pack, or pack the fruit in the freezing container and cover with syrup. Ensure that the fruit remains submerged under syrup for protection by topping with a piece of crumpled foil or wax paper before freezing. Allow headspace in packaging.

SYRUP STRENGTHS

A **light syrup** is made with 2 cups sugar to 4 cups water.

A **medium syrup** is made with 3 cups sugar to 4 cups water.

A **heavy syrup** is made with 4 cups sugar to 4 cups water.

The sugar may be dissolved in hot or cold water but must be chilled before being added to the fruit. It is useful to have a store of syrup in the refrigerator during the fruit-freezing season.

GOLDEN RULES ON FREEZING

1. OBSERVE THE BASIC RULES OF HYGIENE
    The general rule for looking after food is to keep it cool, keep it clean and keep it covered. All raw food should be prepared separately from cooked, ready-to-eat food.

2. FREEZE ONLY TOP QUALITY FOOD
    Freezing can't improve the quality of food and it is a waste of freezer space to store away sub-standard food. Freeze when food is at its peak condition.

3. COOL FOODS QUICKLY
    Cool all food to room temperature or below before putting it into the freezer for the sake of the food already stored there. Use the fast freeze section or fast freeze control to help with this.

4. REMOVE AS MUCH FAT AS POSSIBLE
    Remove as much surplus fat from foods as possible before freezing so that the item does not risk becoming rancid quickly. Drain all fried foods thoroughly on absorbent kitchen paper before freezing to prevent soggy results.

5. USE GOOD EFFECTIVE PACKAGING
    Only use packaging that is guaranteed to be moisture and vapour-

proof. Remove as much air as possible from the packaging used and seal well.

6. LABEL AND DATE PACKAGES
   This will help you to locate food quickly and have a sensible turnover of foods. A record book is a good idea if you are naturally forgetful.

7. OBSERVE STORAGE TIMES
   Don't keep food for longer than the recommended storage times. Use within the periods given for best texture, flavour and nutritional quality.

8. DEFROST ACCORDING TO THE INSTRUCTIONS
   Again follow the recommendations for good results and don't try to unduly hasten the process.

GOLDEN RULES ON RE-FREEZING

The chances of any harmful effect to health in re-freezing are very slight if normal kitchen hygiene rules are obeyed. It is bad practice to defrost and re-freeze foods many times over, for the quality of the food will be affected every time with a proportional deterioration on each occasion.

THE FOLLOWING ARE ACCEPTABLE

* Raw foods from the freezer may be completely cooked and the resultant dish cooled, packed and frozen.

* Those frozen foods which are removed from the freezer for defrosting (especially if in the refrigerator) and are then not required may be put back in the freezer ONLY if some ice can be felt in the pack.

* If a planned food preparation session can be organised with scrupulous kitchen hygiene, the following are all right:

Cream may be defrosted, still in the pack, in the refrigerator until thawed enough to whip to piping thickness. Pipe a selection of rosettes on to a plastic tray, open freeze until solid, then pack, seal, label and return to the freezer.

Pastry may be thawed, still in the wrap, preferably in the refrigerator, until just defrosted enough to roll out. Roll out and make pie crusts, tarts, pastry trimmings etc and re-freeze quickly.

Cakes may be removed from the freezer, decorated whilst still frozen, and returned to the freezer.

THE FOLLOWING ARE NOT RECOMMENDED

* DON'T take out cooked meats, particularly offal, defrost and return it to the freezer, especially if no heat has been applied, as with pâté for example.

* DON'T use frozen shellfish in a cold dish with no cooking, freeze and then return leftovers to the freezer. Eg, lobster mousse.

* What is UNDESIRABLE is to take food from the freezer, leave it hanging around in a warm atmosphere, allow it to come in contact with unclean surfaces, hands, equipment etc, and then return it to the freezer only to freeze-in any contamination that it may have collected during this time. It is fluctuating temperatures that should be avoided; middle temperatures, not hot enough to kill, not cold enough to inactivate the contaminants, are the danger areas.

GOLDEN RULES ON DEFROSTING

Details are included under most individual entries in the A-Z section but here are some general rules and observations:

FRUIT

If this is to be eaten without further cooking, then it is preferable to defrost slowly in the refrigerator and to eat while slightly icy. This may take 6-8 hours or even longer.

If the fruit is to be cooked, if it has been open frozen and is loose, tip straight into a pan, adding sugar to taste and stew very gently over a low heat. Add a little extra water to the pan if the fruit starts to stick. If frozen in syrup and therefore a solid block, place pack under cold water to loosen and then tip into the pan and reheat very gently over a low heat.

VEGETABLES

Cook from frozen. Remember blanching will have par-cooked them and very young, tender vegetables will only require a few minutes; beware of over-cooking.

Alternatively, cook gently from frozen with just a knob of butter added to a covered pan. No water is best or just 15-30 ml/1-2 tablespoons.

Note that it is almost always best to open freeze vegetables in order not to have a solid lump which will be over-cooked on the outside before the inside is defrosted.

STEWS, SAUCES AND SOUPS

Can be cooked from frozen but must be done very gently to prevent sticking. It is preferable to par-defrost in the refrigerator if time is available. A casserole can be reheated from frozen in the oven but stir from time to time to aid defrosting and heating. Sauces and soups can be reheated in a double saucepan. If any separation occurs whisk briskly or liquidise for a few seconds.

CAKES, BREAD AND PASTRY

Cakes will defrost quickly at room temperature, maximum of 2 hours. Remember to remove all wrappings if the cake is decorated.

Bread is best defrosted at room temperature but thawing can be hastened if the loaf is wrapped loosely in foil and placed in a hot oven. Small loaves will defrost in less than 30 minutes like this but large ones tend to remain frozen in the middle after the outside is well defrosted. Bread rolls will defrost and crisp in 10 minutes in a hot oven. Slices of bread from a sliced loaf, if laid out individually, will thaw in a few minutes. Frozen slices can be used directly in a toaster.

Pastry, raw in a piece, will take about 3-4 hours per 450 g/1 lb to defrost at room temperature. Unbaked ready-filled pies should be baked from frozen, allowing about 15 minutes extra cooking time.

POULTRY

All poultry should be fully defrosted before cooking. A bird must be thoroughly cooked to ensure that any harmful bacteria are killed. If a frozen bird is not defrosted there is a real possibility of the outside being well cooked before the inside of the carcass has reached the required temperature. A chicken up to 2 kg/4 lb in weight can take up to 16 hours to defrost in the refrigerator.

FISH

Fillets and steaks cook satisfactorily from frozen but it is preferable to defrost whole or stuffed fish before cooking.
Fish takes quite a long time to defrost – 3 hours per 450 g/1 lb in a refrigerator is a guide. If it is a large pack of solid fish it can take up to 6 hours per 450 g/1 lb.

MEAT

Many people now cook meat from frozen without defrosting first. Steaks, chops and cutlets can be grilled successfully from frozen but it may be difficult to gauge the exact rareness of your steak. They should be cooked at a slightly lower heat for approximately twice the normal time.

Joints should be covered and roasted at 180°C/350°F/Gas 4 for approximately 65 minutes per 450 g/1 lb but a meat thermometer is ideal to ascertain when ready.

It is generally agreed that cooking from frozen reduces shrinkage, moisture loss and flavour loss. Otherwise preferably defrost meat overnight in the refrigerator or in the microwave and cook in the usual way. If you thaw quickly at room temperature and in the microwave there will be a greater loss of moisture but use the drippings or thaw juices to make a sauce or gravy.

A-Z OF BASIC FOODS

ALMOND PASTE

Since almond paste or marzipan has a high oil content it does not freeze very well. Freezer life is short and storage is just as good in the refrigerator or in a cool larder. Cakes, such as wedding or christening cakes covered in almond paste and icing, are still best kept in an airtight tin.

APPLES

Apples of some kind or another are on sale all the year round so they are not worthy of too much freezer space, although a seasonal glut or windfall may entice you to freeze a good quantity of purée and sliced apples for desserts, sauces and baking purposes.

SELECTING FOR FREEZING

There are countless varieties of apples and the choice will be very much a personal one. However, for cooking, Bramley Seedling is an excellent choice and for dessert, consider Cox's Orange Pippin, Laxton's Superb, Discovery, Grenadier, Worcester Pearmain and Egremont Russet – they all freeze superbly. Select good quality apples for freezing that are free from bruising. Best apple bargains tend to be in September and October.

PREPARATION FOR FREEZING

There are several ways to prepare apples for freezing as outlined below. To avoid discolouration when peeling or dicing apples then drop the peeled fruit into a solution of 15 g/½ oz salt to 1 litre/1¾ pints cold water, but do not leave in this solution for longer than 10 minutes. Before blanching or packing rinse in cold water to remove the salt. There is much debate as to whether blanching is necessary for the storage of apples. For short term storage this practise does seem unnecessary but for longer term storage consider the blanching process a must for good results.

TO FREEZE

DRY PACK METHOD: Blanch slices for 1 minute if you like, cool, dry and then open freeze until solid. Pack into rigid containers or polythene bags. Seal, label and freeze.

SUGAR PACK METHOD: Blanch slices for 1 minute if you like, mix slices with sugar using 225 g/8 oz sugar to 1 kg/2 lbs apples. Pack into rigid containers or polythene bags. Seal, label and freeze.

SYRUP PACK METHOD: Use a medium syrup pack for apple slices (see page 25). Slice the apples into rigid containers, cover with syrup and leave a 1.5-2.5 cm/½-1 inch headspace. To keep fruit covered with syrup put crumpled polythene on top. Seal, label and freeze.

PURÉE METHOD: Cook apple slices in the minimum amount of water with or without sugar as you like. Purée in a blender or food processor or pass through a fine nylon sieve and allow to cool. Pack into rigid containers leaving a 2 cm/¾ inch headspace. Seal, label and freeze.

STORAGE TIME: Dry Pack apples for up to 10 months. Sugar Pack, Syrup Pack and Purée for up to 12 months.

TO DEFROST AND SERVE: Leave packs unopened and allow to defrost at room temperature for 1-2 hours. Cook as for fresh apples but do not add any extra liquor.

USES: Use in fruit pies, flans, crumbles, mousses, creams, fruit salads, puddings and tarts. Apples frozen in a dry sugar pack can also be successfully fried to go well with many savoury dishes, especially those with pork or chicken. Apple purée can be used for jellies, mousses and any recipe that calls for puréed apple. It also makes a wonderful accompaniment for pork, duck and goose. Apple purée can be reheated from frozen in a pan over a low heat if it is to be served hot – add a little extra water if necessary during heating to prevent sticking.

APRICOTS

Most of the apricots that we see on sale in Britain come from the Mediterranean although home-grown varieties can be found. The most popular home-grown variety is Moorpark but also consider Hemskerke which can be hardier.

SELECTING FOR FREEZING
Choose firm, ripe, evenly-coloured apricots from late May onwards. There are several methods of freezing but whichever you choose only prepare small quantities at a time to prevent discolouration.

PREPARATION FOR FREEZING
To prepare, wipe, peel if you like but this is not necessary, halve and stone. Brush cut surfaces with lemon juice to prevent turning brown.

TO FREEZE

SUGAR PACK METHOD: Mix apricots with sugar using 225 g/8 oz sugar to 1 kg/2 lbs apricots. Pack into rigid containers or polythene bags. Seal, label and freeze.

SYRUP PACK METHOD: Use a medium syrup pack for apricot halves or slices (see page 25). Slice the apricots or place halves into rigid containers, cover with syrup and leave a 1.5-2.5 cm/½-1 inch headspace. To keep fruit covered put crumpled polythene on top. Seal, label and freeze.

STEWED APRICOT METHOD: Only remove the skins if they are tough, then halve and stone. Poach the fruit until tender with 100 ml/4 fl oz water for every 1 kg/2 lbs fruit, plus sugar to taste. Allow to cool then place in rigid containers leaving a 2 cm/¾ inch headspace. Seal, label and freeze.

PULP OR PURÉE METHOD: Skin the apricots if necessary, then stone and cook them in the minimum amount of water until very tender. Purée in a blender or food processor or pass through a fine nylon sieve. Add sugar later if it is required in a recipe. Pour into rigid containers leaving a 2 cm/¾ inch headspace. Seal, label and freeze.

STORAGE TIME: All methods for up to 12 months.

TO DEFROST AND SERVE: Sugar and Syrup Pack method apricots can be used from frozen for hot puddings and crumbles, or poached in their syrup from frozen. Alternatively, leave in the container in the refrigerator for 3-4 hours before adding to flans, fruit salads and dessert cakes like gâteaux. Stewed apricots can be reheated from frozen over a low heat, stirring frequently to prevent sticking. Add a little extra water if necessary. Apricot pulp should be allowed to thaw at room temperature or in the refrigerator for 2-4 hours until defrosted for use.

USES: Use apricot slices and halves in fruit salads, flans, gâteaux and fruit puddings. Stewed apricots can be used in mousses, creams and fruit desserts. Apricot pulp can be used in mousses, whips, ice creams, cheesecakes, stuffings and sauces.

ARTICHOKES

See *Globe Artichokes* (page 88)
Jerusalem Artichokes (page 98)

ASPARAGUS

Asparagus, by virtue of the fact that it is difficult to grow, is rarely inexpensive. If you are fortunate enough to have a surplus during its short growing season then it is worth freezing to enjoy at other times of the year. Purists would say that only home-grown asparagus is worth freezing, imported has already travelled too far to be fresh enough. However, if you have a good supplier and they can guarantee absolute freshness then go ahead and freeze commercially home-grown and imported asparagus. The official season starts on May 1st and lasts until the end of June but you will undoubtedly see supplies either side of these dates.

SELECTING FOR FREEZING

If you are growing your own then consider the following recommended varieties: Connovers Colossal, Martha Washington, Limburgia and Brocks Imperial. When buying asparagus look for neat bundles with tight heads and tips in which the spears are not too thick. Most are sold by bundle rather than by weight and are graded according to the thickness of the stems. Colour can vary from white to bright green with the whitest stems being the most highly prized (do check however that the stems are not old and woody). 'Sprue' asparagus, the thinnest stemmed variety, can prove to be a good freezer buy since it is cheaper than the thicker varieties and has a good flavour for use in made-up dishes like soups, pies and recipes where appearance isn't paramount.

To prepare, trim off any rough ends and any scales with a sharp knife. Wash thoroughly then sort into piles of a similar thickness and length. For short term storage, asparagus can be frozen unblanched but if freezing for longer than 1 month it should be blanched before freezing.

Blanch small stalks in boiling water for 2 minutes; medium stalks for 3 minutes; large stalks for 4 minutes; and 1 minute for 'sprue' asparagus.

TO FREEZE

Cool quickly, drain and pack neatly in appropriate quantities for use, or lay on a plastic tray in the freezer until solid, then pack in plastic boxes to prevent damage. Seal, label and freeze.

STORAGE TIME: Up to 12 months.

TO DEFROST AND SERVE: If serving whole asparagus hot then always cook from frozen to prevent over-cooking. Plunge into boiling salted water for 2-4 minutes depending upon the thickness of the stems. Drain and serve immediately. For use in made-up dishes, unpack and defrost at room temperature until the stems separate easily then use as for fresh asparagus.

USES: Use asparagus as a starter or vegetable dish with melted butter or hollandaise sauce. Also use for soups, quiches, omelettes, as a filling for tarts, vol-au-vents and soufflés and as a salad ingredient.

ASPIC

It is recommended that dishes coated with aspic are not frozen because aspic does not freeze satisfactorily; it becomes cloudy and dull and separates on defrosting. If a dish, a cooked salmon for example, requires an aspic coating then this is best done after defrosting.

AUBERGINES

Most of the aubergines that we see have been imported, very few are home-grown. The most popular variety looks rather like an overgrown egg with a glossy purple skin. There are however other varieties that can be thin and elongated, or round and stubby, and some have a streaked purple and white skin. If you wish to grow your own then recommended varieties are Long Purple and New York. All aubergine varieties are suitable for freezing.

SELECTING FOR FREEZING
Choose firm, ripe aubergines of uniform size with a rich gloss to the skin; reject those that are wrinkled or dull. Look for specimens that feel 'springy' when lightly pressed. July and August are the best months for bargains at the greengrocer or market.

PREPARATION FOR FREEZING
Young aubergines can be left unpeeled; older ones can be peeled if you like. Cut into cubes or slices about 1.5 cm/½ inch thick, and if preparing large quantities, slice into salted water before blanching, to prevent discolouration. Dégorging - drawing out the bitter juices from the flesh, is now considered unnecessary due to advances in cultivation methods.

TO FREEZE
Immediately after preparation blanch the sliced or diced flesh for 4 minutes in boiling water to which a little lemon juice has been added. Drain, cool quickly in iced water, then drain again thoroughly and pat dry with absorbent kitchen paper. Open freeze slices until solid, then pack in polythene bags or rigid containers, separating the layers with interleaving sheets or foil. Seal, label and freeze. Diced aubergine cubes can be packed straight into polythene bags without open freezing. Seal, label and freeze.

STORAGE TIME: Up to 9 months.

TO DEFROST AND SERVE: Leave to thaw in the wrappings at room temperature until just beginning to soften, then dry as much as possible with absorbent kitchen paper. Fry in oil or butter for about 5 minutes.

USES: Use as a vegetable cooked in butter or oil or combined with other ingredients to make a ratatouille, moussaka or vegetarian curry.

AVOCADOS

Avocados do not freeze successfully as whole pears but the flesh can be used in made-up dishes like mousses, soups and ice creams and frozen. Alternatively, the flesh can be pulped and frozen and used later in made-up dishes after defrosting.

SELECTING FOR FREEZING

Look out for low-priced imported bargains during July and August. Ideal fruit for freezing should be just ripe. Avoid over-ripe specimens and allow under-ripe ones to ripen further before preparation.

PREPARATION FOR FREEZING

Skin and stone the avocado then blend or sieve with lemon juice to prevent discolouration. Allow 15 ml/1 tablespoon lemon juice for each avocado. Add any seasonings after defrosting.

TO FREEZE

Pack as soon as possible in a rigid container. Seal, label and freeze.

STORAGE TIME: Up to 2 months.

TO DEFROST AND SERVE: Leave to stand in a covered container at room temperature for 2 hours. Stir well and use immediately.

USES: Use in dips, soups, sauces, cheesecakes, mousses and made-up dishes.

BACON

Because bacon is a cured meat and because of its relatively high fat content it does not keep as well as fresh meat over a long period of time in the freezer. It is quite satisfactory however over short periods.

SELECTING FOR FREEZING

Choose only really fresh bacon, which should have a pleasant smell with lean, pink flesh and white, firm fat. Endeavour to tell your supplier where possible that you wish to freeze the rashers or joints he supplies so that he can inform you of the day he receives it fresh from the wholesaler.

PREPARATION FOR FREEZING

Cut joints to the size most suitable for your needs. Sort steaks, rashers and bacon chops according to use in cooking and in quantities suitable to your needs, probably 225 g/8 oz packs.

TO FREEZE

Wrap closely in freezer foil and then in a polythene bag, excluding as much air as possible. Vacuum packing of bacon considerably extends the storage life in the freezer because the air, which promotes rancidity, has been extracted from the packet. Check if the bacon you are supplied with is vacuum packed or not before purchase and freezing. Vacuum packs should be carefully checked to make sure that the pack has not been damaged. Wrap the vacuum pack in a polythene freezer bag or foil, seal, label and freeze. This outer wrapper will protect the vacuum as some packs can become very brittle at freezer temperatures and can puncture very easily.

Cooked bacon joints or leftovers of a cooked joint can be frozen, but as the flavour changes and drying out takes place more quickly than with raw bacon the storage time is considerably shorter. Wrap tightly in foil and place in a polythene bag, exclude as much air as possible, seal, label and freeze.

STORAGE TIMES: Smoked bacon joints up to 8 weeks; unsmoked bacon joints up to 5 weeks; smoked rashers, chops and gammon steaks up to 8 weeks; unsmoked rashers, chops and gammon steaks up to 3 weeks; vacuum-packed bacon joints (smoked and unsmoked) up to 20 weeks or as recommended by supplier; vacuum-packed rashers or steaks (smoked or unsmoked) up to 20 weeks or as recommended by supplier and freezer packs of Danepack Danish bacon up to 25 weeks. Cooked joints of bacon and leftovers should be used within 4 weeks.

TO DEFROST AND SERVE: Bacon Joints: Allow bacon plenty of time to thaw slowly in a cool place. This is important because the more slowly the meat is thawed, the better the quality will be when cooked. Defrosting in the refrigerator is recommended because the cool temperature will continue to preserve the maximum freshness of the meat. The wrapping material should be opened on removal from the freezer. Remove any wrappings completely as soon as possible during the defrosting process.

Bacon Rashers and Pieces: Packets of bacon rashers, steaks, chops and small pieces may be thawed overnight in the refrigerator or, if for immediate use, can be thawed in hot water for a few minutes. Dry them well on absorbent kitchen paper before frying or grilling.

Frozen bacon should be cooked immediately it has defrosted for best results.

DO NOT RE-FREEZE RAW BACON AFTER DEFROSTING.

USES: As a main course or buffet dish served hot with an onion or parsley sauce; as a cold dish served with pickles and relishes; grilled or fried rashers for breakfast-style platters or sandwiches; as an ingredient for quiches, flans, stuffings, sauces, hot pots and casseroles; grilled steaks and chops with a tart fruit garnish like apple or pineapple; and as a garnish for roast chicken and turkey.

BANANAS

Although available all year round, bananas are at their best and at their cheapest during spring and early summer. Although they cannot be frozen whole in their skins, bananas can be frozen in a pulp form and in made-up dishes like cakes, fools, teabreads and, of course, baby food.

SELECTING FOR FREEZING

Choose firm, ripe fruit with deep yellow skins and just a few spots of brown, indicating they are in peak condition. If in doubt choose under-ripe rather than over-ripe fruit and ripen in a dry warm place for a few days.

PREPARATION FOR FREEZING

To freeze as a pulp, peel and immediately mash with lemon juice and sugar to taste. Generally, allow 45 ml/3 tablespoons lemon juice and 100 g/4 oz sugar for every 6-8 bananas, depending upon size.

TO FREEZE

Pack immediately in usable quantities in rigid containers, leaving a 2 cm/¾ inch headspace. Seal, label and freeze.

STORAGE TIME: Up to 6 months.

TO DEFROST AND SERVE: Thaw banana pulp in its container in the refrigerator for 5-6 hours. Use immediately after opening the container.

USES: As an ingredient for a teabread or loaf; for making breads, cakes or whipped desserts; and as a sandwich filling.

BASS

Bass is a sea fish usually weighing about ½-3½ kg/1-8 lbs. It is in season from June to March. It has a delicate flesh which is firm, lean and pink in colour.

SELECTING FOR FREEZING

Choose fish that is really fresh, ideally within 12 hours of the catch. Fresh fish can be recognised by its firm flesh, clear, full and shiny eyes and clean smell. Steaks, cutlets and fillets should have firm, closely packed flakes; any with a watery or fibrous appearance are stale.

PREPARATION FOR FREEZING

Clean and gut fish, then fillet, cut into steaks or, if small, leave whole. Rinse under cold running water and pat dry with absorbent kitchen paper.

TO FREEZE

Wrap individual whole fish in cling film, then overwrap in polythene bags. Exclude as much air as possible and seal. Interleave steaks and fillets, then pack together in bags. Seal, label and freeze.

STORAGE TIME: Up to 3 months.

TO DEFROST AND SERVE: Thaw whole fish in wrappings in the refrigerator overnight then cook as fresh. Cook steaks and fillets from frozen as for commercially frozen fish.

USES: Bass is suitable for poaching, baking, barbecuing or grilling.

BEANS

See *Broad Beans* (page 47)
   French beans (page 86)
   Runner Beans (page 143)

BEEF

For the home-freezer owner it is usual to buy either a quarter of a beast (fore or hind) or a range of already jointed chosen cuts (a 14 kg/30 lb pack of individual roasting cuts, for example). The latter method is usually more expensive per kg/lb but you are getting just what you want ready prepared and there is no wastage for unwanted bone or fat, etc. When buying the complete quarter the price per kg/lb, quoted includes bones and fat that will be trimmed away by the butcher and therefore the net price per kg/lb of meat actually put into the freezer will be more than the initial price quoted. Also you have to take all the cuts obtained from that particular section, which may include some you would not normally use. This is not to say that the cheaper braising and stewing cuts are not excellent value but you do have to be an imaginative cook in using them all to get the full benefit of a bulk buy.

SELECTING FOR FREEZING

The colour of beef does not really give any guide to its quality. When beef is freshly cut it will be bright red, but on exposure to air it changes fairly quickly to brownish red. Therefore a bright red colour is no indication of better eating quality. The fat of a beast also differs in colour from yellow to white, which is dependent on the type of feed the animal has received. Whilst a little fat on a joint is beneficial for cooking and to produce a good flavour, do avoid those that are over-fatty in appearance.

BUYING A BEEF HINDQUARTER:The hindquarter is where you find the top quality meat for roasting and grilling. Cuts obtained are sirloin, fillet, rump, topside, silverside, top rump, leg, flank and skirt.

The average size of a hindquarter is about 70-80 kg/145-170 lbs. There are several different ways of cutting the meat and careful discussion with your supplier will ensure that you get just what you want (for example tell him just how thick you want your steaks, what weight you want the joints to be etc).

BUYING A BEEF FOREQUARTER:The forequarter is the section which includes meat more suitable for slower methods of cooking, eg braising, pot roasting, stewing and casseroling. The average size of a forequarter of beef is 65-70 kg/135-145 lbs. Cuts that this would yield include foreribs, backribs, topribs, chuck and blade, neck and clod, shin, brisket and flank. Here again, there are different ways of butchering and do make sure that your butcher knows your requirements (for example do you want the blade cubed for casseroles, cut into slices for braising or left in joints for pot-roasting or braising).

PREPARATION FOR FREEZING AND TO FREEZE

JOINTS (for roasting/slow roasting/pot roasting/braising from both forequarter and hindquarter): Saw off any protruding bone ends and remove any surplus fat. Pad bones with foil. Do not stuff boned and rolled joints. Wrap individual joints in cling film or foil, then overwrap in polythene bags. Exclude as much air as possible. Seal, label and freeze.

STEAKS (for grilling/frying/barbecuing from both the forequarter and hindquarter): Remove any surplus fat. Ideally do not cut more than 2.5 cm/1 inch thick. Pad any protruding bones on forerib steaks with foil. Wrap individually in cling film or foil and interleave. Pack together in polythene bags. Exclude as much air as possible. Seal, label and freeze.

SLICES AND CUBES (for braising/casseroling/pies/stewing from both the forequarter and hindquarter): Trim off surplus fat, sinews and gristle. Cut into 2.5 cm/1 inch thick slices or cubes if not already done. Pack in usable quantities in polythene bags. Exclude as much air as possible. Seal, label and freeze.

MINCED BEEF (from forequarter and hindquarter meat): Only freeze lean minced meat. Leave loose or shape into burgers, meatballs, patties etc. Pack loose mince in usable quantities in polythene bags. Exclude as much air as possible. Seal, label and freeze. To freeze burgers, patties and meatballs see BURGERS (page 50).

STORAGE TIME: Joints for up to 12 months; steaks for up to 12 months; slices and cubes for up to 8 months; minced beef for up to 3 months.

TO DEFROST AND SERVE

JOINTS: Defrost in the wrappings at room temperature for 6-8 hours per kg/3-4 hours per lb, then cook as for fresh. Small joints under 1.5 kg/3 lbs and on the bone can be cooked from frozen for approximately twice the usual time until 74°C/165°F is registered on a meat thermometer. Do not cook boned and rolled joints from frozen.

STEAKS: Thaw in the wrappings at room temperature for 2-3 hours or in the refrigerator overnight, then cook as for fresh. Or grill/fry thin steaks from frozen; allow extra time and brush well with oil.

SLICES AND CUBES: Thaw in the wrappings at room temperature until pieces separate, then cook as for fresh, allowing a little extra time and using thawed juices.

MINCED BEEF: Partially defrost loose mince in wrappings in the refrigerator, then cook as for fresh, stirring well to prevent sticking. Cook burgers, meatballs etc from frozen.

USES: Beef can be cooked by almost every method including roasting, braising, frying, grilling, casseroling, barbecuing, pot-roasting, stir-frying and stewing.

BEEFBURGERS

See *Burgers* (page 50)

BEETROOT

Red or globe is the most common beetroot grown for eating. One of the easiest vegetables to grow, it is worth freezing if you have a bumper crop in the garden or see young springtime beetroot at a good price in the shops or market.

SELECTING FOR FREEZING

Harvest young beetroot from the garden in springtime when they are no more than 7.5 cm/3 inches in diameter. Alternatively, look for commercially grown beetroot bargains towards the end of May. Buy fresh and uncooked beets with the leaves still attached (these should be crisp and green, avoid those with limp or yellow leaves, they are undoubtedly stale). For best results buy small young beets that are even-sized and spherical, they freeze better than the long and tapering main crop varieties.

PREPARATION FOR FREEZING

Twist off the leaves (do not cut or they will 'bleed' during cooking). Wash carefully in cold water and always cook before freezing. To cook, place in a pan of cold water with 5 ml/1 tsp vinegar. Add 1-2 bay leaves and a few black peppercorns, if you like, for extra flavour. Bring to the boil, reduce the heat, cover and simmer for 10-20 minutes, according to size, until tender. Drain thoroughly, rinse under cold running water then rub off the skins with your fingers. Leave until cold but do not soak.

TO FREEZE

Pack whole, cooked beetroot into rigid containers rather than plastic bags; larger beetroot can be sliced or diced before packing if preferred. Seal, label and freeze.

STORAGE TIME: Freeze for up to 6 months.

TO DEFROST AND SERVE: Defrost beetroot in its container for at least 4 hours at room temperature before using.

USES: Use cold in salads (oranges are a good accompaniment); serve hot as a vegetable with a béchamel, light horseradish or seasoned crème fraîche sauce; add to stews and casseroles for colour; or make into a tasty hot or cold soup, for example, Bortsch.

BISCUITS

Most baked biscuits store for a considerable length of time in a tightly sealed tin, therefore it is often unnecessary to freeze these. However, there are times when a batch copes with an unexpected emergency. Consider therefore freezing these both baked or better still unbaked.

SELECTING FOR FREEZING

Unbaked biscuit mixtures containing over 100 g/4 oz fat to 450g/1 lb flour freeze satisfactorily. Biscuits which have been cut out are difficult to store without damage and the easiest way to freeze the mixture is in rolls of the same diameter as the required biscuit. Several different flavours can be made from one large batch of mixture. Soft mixtures can be piped or spooned before freezing.

PREPARATION FOR FREEZING AND TO FREEZE

Prepare the dough as per recipe then form into rolls about the same diameter as the required biscuit. Wrap each roll individually in polythene bags. Seal, label and freeze.

Pipe or spoon soft biscuit mixtures onto a baking tray and open freeze until solid. When frozen lift off the tray with a palette knife and pack into polythene bags or rigid containers in usable quantities. Seal, label and return to the freezer.

Pack cooked biscuits into rigid containers in usable quantities. Seal, label and freeze. A good and useful tip is to store such fragile items in a very well washed washing-up liquid container. Cut off the top and seal with freezer tape to make a lid. Label and freeze.

STORAGE TIME: Up to 6 months.

TO DEFROST AND SERVE: Leave rolls of biscuit mixture in their wrapping at room temperature until sufficiently soft to cut into thin slices. Bake as usual.

Place frozen piped or spooned biscuits onto a baking tray and bake at the usual temperature, allowing about 5 minutes longer than normal.

Leave cooked biscuits to stand in their wrappings at room temperature for 20-30 minutes to defrost. Serve as soon as possible.

USES: As a tea-time and coffee-time treat; for making bases for cheesecakes; and for layering with fruit and cream in desserts.

BLACKBERRIES

Home-freezer enthusiasts can choose from both wild and cultivated blackberries for freezing.

SELECTING FOR FREEZING

Cultivated blackberries are available from markets and pick-your-own farms from late July to mid-September. Wild blackberries, depending upon the weather, ripen from early August onwards. Choose berries that are ripe with a rich black colour. Reject those with traces of red but also avoid those that are squashy and over-ripe. If the fruit is pre-packaged then avoid those with any signs of mould or where there are signs of leakage from the base. If picking your own do so when the weather conditions are dry and try to avoid those fruits that look dirty, especially roadside specimens that might contain a high degree of lead.

PREPARATION FOR FREEZING
Blackberries can be frozen whole or as a purée. Whole blackberries should be washed and any stalks should be removed. Pat dry with absorbent kitchen paper.

Blackberry purée should be made by cooking the fruit in the minimum amount of water with sugar to taste until tender. Pass through a sieve, or purée in a blender or food processor then sieve to remove any pips.

TO FREEZE
Whole blackberries can be frozen whole in free-flow packs; whole in a dry sugar pack; or in a sugar syrup pack.

To make a free-flow pack, open freeze on trays until solid. Pack in usable quantities in polythene bags. Seal, label and return to the freezer.

To make a dry sugar pack, pack the berries in usable quantities in rigid containers, sprinkling each layer with sugar and allowing 100-175 g/ 4-6 oz sugar to every 450 g/1 lb fruit, according to taste. Seal, label and freeze.

To make a sugar syrup pack, pack the berries in usable quantities in rigid containers and cover with a medium sugar syrup (see page 25). Leave a 2 cm/¾ inch headspace. Seal, label and freeze.

Blackberry purée should be poured in usable quantities into rigid containers, leaving a 2 cm/¾ inch headspace. Seal, label and freeze.

STORAGE TIME: Whole berries prepared by any of the above methods up to 12 months; blackberry purée for up to 8 months.

TO DEFROST AND SERVE: Leave whole blackberries frozen raw or in a dry sugar pack to defrost in their wrappings at room temperature for 2-3 hours, or transfer to a bowl and leave for 1½-2 hours. Blackberries frozen in syrup can be reheated gently from frozen but should be stirred frequently. Blackberry purée should be left to stand at room temperature in its container for 2-3 hours.

USES: Use whole blackberries for fruit salads, pies and crumbles, summer puddings, jams, jellies and other preserves or for eating raw with fresh cream. Blackberry purée can be used in ice creams, sorbets and mousses or to make a sauce for serving with desserts.

BLACK PUDDING

Old-fashioned black pudding are regaining popularity with the interest in traditional British food.

SELECTING FOR FREEZING

Buy from a reputable supplier and never bulk buy unless you have tasted the pudding first. Make sure your butcher, grocer or supplier knows that you intend to freeze your supply so that you have a fresh delivery and that the puddings have not already been frozen.

TO FREEZE

Wrap each individual black pudding, or slices from a large one, in cling film or freezer wrap and place all portions in a polythene bag for freezing. Seal, label and freeze.

STORAGE TIME: Freeze for 1-2 months.

USES: Delicious boiled and served with a mustard sauce or sliced and fried with bacon for a breakfast dish. Fried apple slices also make a good tart accompaniment.

BLUEBERRIES

This small, dark blue fruit is in season in mid-summer. It can be eaten fresh or stewed with sugar. It can also be cooked in pies, muffins, desserts or made into preserves. Treat in the same way as blackcurrants for freezing.

For freezing follow the instructions for freezing CURRANTS (see page 76).

BRAWN

Preparing brawn from a pig's head produces a tasty dish which freezes well.

SELECTING FOR FREEZING

Any recipe chosen for preparing brawn that is to be frozen should have slightly less seasoning than if to be eaten fresh as the seasonings intensify during freezer storage.

PREPARATION FOR FREEZING

Unless preparing in a large tin for a party, freeze in small containers for individual use.

TO FREEZE

Freeze in the tin or remove from the tin to freeze as you like. Interleave slices then overwrap in polythene or foil. Seal, label and freeze.

STORAGE TIME: Up to 2 months.

TO DEFROST AND SERVE: Defrost overnight in the wrappings in the refrigerator.

USES: Use in sandwiches, snacks and salads.

BREAD

BAKED BREAD

All baked bread, whether bought or home-made, freezes well, providing it is freshly baked when frozen.

PREPARATION FOR FREEZING AND TO FREEZE

Wrap in heavy-duty foil or polythene bags. Commercially sliced loaves can be stored in their own waxed paper wrapper or polythene bags. Seal, label and freeze.

STORAGE TIME: White and brown bread can be frozen for up to 6 months; enriched bread and rolls (milk, fruit, malt loaves and soft rolls) for up to 4 months; crisp-crusted loaves and rolls have a limited storage time as the crusts begin to shell off after 1 week; Vienna-type loaves and rolls keep for only about 3 days in the freezer.

TO DEFROST AND SERVE: Leave rolls in their packaging at room temperature for 3-6 hours, depending upon the size of the loaf, or leave overnight in the refrigerator. Alternatively, place a frozen loaf, wrapped in foil, in a fairly hot oven, 200°C/400°F/Gas 6, and cook for 45 minutes.
    Sliced bread can be toasted from frozen. Sliced loaves will defrost quickly at room temperature if the slices are laid out separately. A thin-sliced loaf prepared this way will defrost in about 5-10 minutes.
    Place frozen rolls wrapped in foil in a very hot oven, 230°C/450°F/Gas 8, for 15 minutes, or leave in their packaging at room temperature for 1½ hours.
    Ideally crusty loaves and rolls defrosted at room temperature should be refreshed before serving. Place unwrapped loaves or rolls in a fairly hot oven, 200°C/400°F/Gas 6, for 5-10 minutes.

USES: For serving with soups, pâtés, preserves and spreads. For serving as a starter, main course and snack accompaniment. For making sandwiches and filled rolls. For making herb and garlic-flavoured bread. For lining a basin for a summer pudding.

PAR-BAKED BREAD

Both home-baked white and wheatmeal rolls can be frozen partly baked. This is a very successful method, as the frozen rolls can be put straight from the freezer into the oven to finish baking; ideal for serving for breakfast. Loaves are not so successful as rolls because during par-baking the crust becomes well formed and coloured before the centre of the loaf is set. Par-baked loaves and rolls available in shops also freeze well.

PREPARATION FOR FREEZING

To par-bake rolls, place the shaped and risen rolls in a very hot oven, 230°C/450°F/Gas 8, for 5 minutes, reduce the oven temperature to cool, 150°C/300°F/Gas 2, and bake for a further 10 minutes. The rolls must be set, but still pale in colour. Cool.

TO FREEZE

Pack cooled rolls in usable quantities in heavy-duty foil or polythene bags. Seal, label and freeze.

STORAGE TIME: Up to 4 months for home-made par-baked rolls; up to 2 months for commercially prepared par-baked rolls.

TO DEFROST AND SERVE: Unwrap and place frozen par-baked rolls in the oven to defrost and complete baking. Bake white rolls at 200°C, 400°F/Gas 6 for 20 minutes. Bake brown rolls at 230°C/450°F/Gas 8 for 20 minutes.

USES: As for baked bread above.

BREADCRUMBS

Infinitely useful, a store of ready-prepared breadcrumbs in the freezer can save considerable time when preparing countless dishes like stuffings and sauces.

SELECTING FOR FREEZING

Undoubtedly plain white breadcrumbs are the most useful type to freeze but also consider wheatmeal, wholemeal and flavoured breadcrumbs for both sweet and savoury dishes.

PREPARATION FOR FREEZING AND TO FREEZE

Prepare by hand using a grater or prepare in a food processor or blender. Pack into polythene bags or a rigid container. Seal, label and freeze.

STORAGE TIME: Up to 3 months.

TO DEFROST AND USE: Breadcrumbs need not be defrosted for use in stuffings, puddings and sauces. To use for coatings, leave at room temperature for 30 minutes.

USES: For stuffings, sauces, coatings, toppings for gratins, fillings for puddings and fried in butter for serving with game birds.

BREAM

Bream is a fresh-water fish weighing from ½-1½ kg/1-3 lbs. It is in season from June until March. For freezing whole large fish follow the instructions for freezing SALMON (page 144).

For freezing small whole fish follow the instructions for TROUT (page 163).

BRILL

Brill is a fresh-water flat fish caught in the North Sea, Mediterranean, and Black Sea. It is cooked in the same way as sole and turbot. It is in season from September to May.

For freezing follow the instructions for freezing COD (page 69).

BROAD BEANS

Broad beans can be one of the very earliest home-grown vegetables to appear after the winter months and are especially delicious if picked or bought when young, small and very fresh. Older beans, left too long in the pod, are invariably leathery and floury.

SELECTING FOR FREEZING

Choose pods which are young and small; reject any beans which appear starchy. Very young beans can be eaten still in the pod but sadly this is only really an option for the kitchen gardener since most beans sold are too mature and must be shelled for eating.

PREPARATION FOR FREEZING

Wash beans still in their pods that are intended for eating that way under cold running water. If freezing shelled beans, remove from the pods and grade according to size.

TO FREEZE

Sort pods into usable quantities of the same size then blanch in boiling water (to which a little lemon juice has been added) for 2 minutes. Drain, cool quickly in iced water. Drain again and pat dry with absorbent kitchen paper. Pack into polythene bags, seal, label and freeze. Shelled beans should be blanched in boiling water for 1½ minutes. Drain, cool quickly in iced water. Drain again and pat dry with absorbent kitchen paper. Open freeze on trays until solid. Pack in usable quantities in polythene bags, seal, label and freeze.

STORAGE TIME: Up to 12 months.

TO DEFROST AND SERVE: Never thaw pods or shelled beans before cooking. Add to boiling, salted water and cook for 3-5 minutes, depending upon size.

USES: Serve hot as a vegetable accompaniment tossed in melted butter with herbs if you like. Broad beans are also delicious if cooked and served in a parsley or light mustard sauce. Cooked beans are also good in spring mixture salads (toss while still warm in the dressing for maximum flavour absorption). Broad beans can also be used to make soups, gratins, curries and for serving with pasta.

BROCCOLI

Calabrese or purple sprouting broccoli is perhaps the only variety of broccoli that freezes well. The remaining varieties do not give good results after defrosting. They can however be frozen for use in a soup or as a purée mixture for a vegetable terrine.

For freezing follow the instructions for freezing CALABRESE (page 54).

BRUSSELS SPROUTS

Brussels sprouts are excellent for freezing and so are worth buying in bulk, especially the small button ones.

SELECTING FOR FREEZING

Choose small, very firm and tight-headed sprouts for freezing. Reject any that are yellowing or have loose heads.

PREPARATION FOR FREEZING

Wash well, trim the bases and remove any damaged or loose outer leaves. Grade for size. Do not be tempted to put a cross in the base. Any larger sprouts can be frozen as a purée. Cook in boiling salted water until just tender, then drain and purée in a blender or food processor until smooth.

TO FREEZE

Whole sprouts need to be blanched in boiling water for 1½-3 minutes, depending upon size. Drain and cool in iced water, drain again and pat dry with absorbent kitchen paper. Open freeze until solid then pack into polythene bags or rigid containers. Seal, label and return to the freezer. Pack sprout purée, in usable quantities, in rigid containers. Seal, label and freeze.

STORAGE TIME: Up to 12 months.

TO DEFROST AND SERVE: Cook whole sprouts from frozen in boiling salted water for 5-7 minutes, depending upon size. Reheat sprout purée from frozen over a very low heat, adding a little extra water to prevent sticking if necessary.

USES: As a vegetable accompaniment. Whole cooked sprouts can be tossed in butter with a little grated nutmeg and seasoning to taste. For variety add a few cooked chestnuts or pieces of crisply grilled bacon. Alternatively coat in a white or cheese sauce and sprinkle with breadcrumbs to make a gratin. Sprout purée is ideal for making soups or mixtures for vegetable terrines.

BUCKLING

Buckling is also known as the Baltic Herring and is imported into this country generally in its smoked state. It is very rarely available for home freezing in its fresh state.

SELECTING FOR FREEZING

As buckling the herring is brined before smoking and is available for retail sale and commercially frozen. Do make sure it is quite freshly received from the smokers if it is to be home frozen.

PREPARATION FOR FREEZING

No special preparation is required. Wrap in cling film then in polythene bags. Exclude as much air as possible. Seal, label and freeze.

STORAGE TIME: Up to 2 months.

TO DEFROST AND SERVE: Defrost in the wrappings in the refrigerator overnight.

USES: Serve as an hors d'oeuvres or use to make a delicious pâté which stores well in the freezer.

BURGERS

Many burgers from beef, lamb, pork and chicken to vegetable-based and soya are readily available commercially in varying sizes, thicknesses and quality for the home freezer. However, they are useful to prepare at home if large quantities of minced meat are available or a special recipe is liked.

SELECTING FOR FREEZING

Obviously it makes sense only to buy in quantity those burgers that your family has already tasted and liked and whose quality you are assured is first class. If you are making up burgers from a recipe then try out a small batch first before committing yourself to a bulk buy and preparation session. If long term storage is your priority then choose a recipe that is not highly seasoned since seasonings can reduce the storage time to only 4-6 weeks, whereas plain burgers with just a hint of seasoning have a storage life of up to 3 months.

PREPARATION FOR FREEZING

If you are making burgers in bulk and regularly serve such fare then consider buying a burger press. These help in giving a good compact round burger shape.

TO FREEZE

Freeze individually by open freezing on a tray. Pack in usable quantities, interleaving between each burger with polythene sheets, cling film or foil (use a double layer of cling film so that they can be separated when frozen). Seal, label and return to the freezer.

STORAGE TIME: 4-6 weeks for highly-seasoned burgers; up to 3 months for unseasoned burgers.

USES: Grill, bake or fry and serve with grills, in buns with salad and relishes, or as a main course meal with salad and jacket potatoes or fries.

BUTTER AND FLAVOURED BUTTERS

SELECTING FOR FREEZING

Farm-fresh butter and butter at a special offer price is worth freezing but, if buying from a shop, make sure it is a fresh stock and, if from a farm, that it has been made from pasteurised cream. Also make a note of whether the butter is salted or unsalted since the storage times differ appreciably. Flavoured butters should be frozen very quickly after making to ensure good eating quality at a later date.

PREPARATION FOR FREEZING

Freeze as soon as possible after purchase. Freeze in 225 g/8 oz quantities. Flavoured butter (lemon, garlic, maître d'hôtel, devilled and herb for example) should be prepared then chilled until it can be formed into a long sausage shape of suitable diameter for slicing and presentation, about 4 cm/1½ inches in diameter. Roll inside a sheet of wet freezer film so that it does not stick. When firm cut into slices and re-form the roll with film dividers between the slices.

TO FREEZE

Leave plain butter in its original packaging then overwrap in foil or a freezer bag. Seal, label and freeze.

Pack flavoured butter slices in a polythene bag or stack in rigid plastic tumblers for easy dispensing. Seal, label and freeze.

STORAGE TIME: Plain, unsalted butter can be frozen for up to 6 months. Plain, salted butter can be frozen for up to 3 months. Flavoured butters (other than garlic) can be frozen for up to 3 months. Garlic butter should not be frozen for any longer than 1 month.

TO DEFROST AND SERVE: Remove any overwrapping from plain butter and defrost in the refrigerator for about 4 hours or at room temperature for about 2 hours. Flavoured butters can generally be used straight from the freezer.

USES: Plain butter can be used as a spread, cooking fat for frying and sautéeing and as a sealing agent on pâtés and potted dishes like meat and fish. Flavoured butters can be used to make garlic and herb breads, savoury and sweet sandwiches, as an accompaniment to grilled meats and fish and basting agent for roasts and barbecued food.

CABBAGE

HARD RED AND WHITE

Both hard red and white cabbage are suitable for freezing. Red cabbage is on the market from autumn onwards and is well worth buying or harvesting from your kitchen garden well before the worst of the winter weather, since it can be damaged by severe frost.

Since cabbages are readily available all year in one type or another they do not merit too much freezer space but are convenient ready sliced or in made-up dishes like a red cabbage and apple mixture.

SELECTING FOR FREEZING

Prepare cabbages within 24 hours of picking or harvesting for prime freshness. Select good firm specimens of the type your family prefers. Red cabbages should have a bluish bloom to their outer leaves while the inner heart should be a shiny purple.

White cabbage should also be firm and have a crisp white casing of leaves for the inner section. Choose cabbages that are heavy for their size to ensure compactness.

PREPARATION FOR FREEZING

Remove and discard the outer leaves. Cut the cabbage into quarters, remove the woody stem and shred finely.

TO FREEZE

Blanch in boiling water for 1 minute, drain, cool in iced water, drain again and pat dry with absorbent kitchen paper. Pack in usable quantities in polythene bags. Seal, label and freeze.

STORAGE TIME: Up to 12 months.

TO DEFROST AND SERVE: Cook both red and white cabbage from frozen in boiling salted water for 5 minutes until just tender. Alternatively, defrost in their wrappings at room temperature for 1-2 hours then braise in the oven.

USES: Serve as a vegetable accompaniment with butter and seasonings. Braised white and red cabbage makes an excellent meal accompaniment. Consider braising red cabbage with apples, onions and red wine and braise white cabbage with caraway seeds, onions and perhaps garlic.

SPRING CABBAGE

There are so many different types of cabbages available all year round that it doesn't seem worthwhile to freeze a great deal. However, if spring cabbage is a real favourite, this is the best way to preserve it.

SELECTING FOR FREEZING

There are basically two types: spring greens which are young, unhearted cabbages, and spring cabbage which is the hearted variety. Young hearted cabbages are most successful in the freezer. Choose the best quality, freshest looking cabbages that do not show any signs of wilting.

PREPARATION FOR FREEZING

Do not freeze as whole cabbages. Separate the leaves from the cabbage and wash under cold running water. Trim the stalks, cutting off any hard ends. Leave whole or cut the leaves into strips about 1 cm/½ inch wide.

TO FREEZE

Blanch in boiling water to which 15-30 ml/1-2 tablespoons vinegar have been added (to retain colour) for 1½ minutes. Drain, cool quickly in iced water, drain again throughly. Pack in usable quantities in polythene bags. Double wrapping is often advisable to prevent cabbage odour tainting other food in the freezer. Seal, label and freeze.

STORAGE TIME: Up to 6 months.

TO DEFROST AND SERVE: Frozen spring cabbage must be cooked after freezing and should not be thawed after freezing either unless you intend to stuff the whole leaves (see below). Cook in boiling salted water, uncovered, for 5 minutes, stirring frequently. Drain to serve.

USES: As a vegetable accompaniment with butter and pepper. Defrosted whole leaves can be stuffed with meat, rice or vegetable mixtures, then rolled and baked in the oven. Delicious if served with a tomato and onion sauce.

CAKES

—— BAKED, DECORATED AND UNDECORATED ——

Most baked cakes freeze well whether rich or plain, decorated or not. As rich cakes keep well in airtight tins there is little point in freezing them. Swiss rolls, whisked sponges and sponge flan cases which go stale quickly after baking are particularly good to freeze.

PREPARATION FOR FREEZING AND TO FREEZE

Wrap cooled undecorated cakes in polythene bags or place in rigid containers. Seal, label and freeze.

Decorated cakes should be placed on a tray and frozen until solid. When solid wrap in polythene bags or in a rigid container. Boxes are invariably better than bags since they offer more protection.

STORAGE TIME: Undecorated cakes for up to 6 months; decorated cakes for up to 3 months.

TO DEFROST AND SERVE: Leave undecorated cakes to defrost in their packaging at room temperature. Small cakes take about 1 hour, larger cakes 2-3 hours, sponge cakes and flans 1½-2 hours and a Swiss roll about 2-2½ hours.

Decorated cakes should be unwrapped and placed on their serving platter and left to defrost at room temperature for 2-4 hours, depending upon size. A useful tip is to put the cake on the lid and cover with the container rather than inside the container, for easy removal after freezing, especially decorated cakes.

UNCOOKED CAKE MIXTURES

Rich creamed mixtures, like Victoria sandwich mix, freeze satisfactorily. Whisked sponge mixtures do not freeze well before cooking. Rich cake mixtures may be frozen in two ways. In a greased foil-lined tin or in a foil cake tin. Place the mixture uncovered in a foil-lined tin or foil case. Remove from the tin when solid and wrap in heavy-duty foil. If in a foil tin, cover with a lid or foil. Seal, label and freeze.

Pack uncooked cake mixture in a polythene box or carton. Seal, label and freeze.

STORAGE TIME: Up to 2 months.

TO DEFROST AND USE: Defrost uncooked cake mixtures other than rich, at room temperature for 2-3 hours, then use as required for cakes, small puddings and large cakes. To use uncooked rich cake mixtures, return the frozen mixture to the greased original tin or uncover the foil dish, then cook from frozen at the normal temperature, allowing 5 minutes extra cooking time.

USES: For cakes, buns, puddings and flan cases.

CALABRESE

Also known as purple-sprouting broccoli. This is the only type of broccoli that really freezes well.

SELECTING FOR FREEZING
Pick or buy only best quality calabrese for freezing. The stalks should not be any more than 2.5 cm/1 inch thick and should show no signs of wilting, yellowing or damage.

PREPARATION FOR FREEZING
Cut away outer leaves and trim any thick or woody stems. Wash thoroughly in salted water, then rinse under cold running water. Grade according to thickness.

TO FREEZE
Blanch before freezing, thick stems need 4 minutes, medium stems 3 minutes and thin stems 2 minutes in boiling water. Drain, cool quickly in iced water, drain again and pat dry with absorbent kitchen paper. Pack into rigid containers, alternating the heads top to bottom. Seal, label and freeze.

STORAGE TIME: Up to 12 months.

TO DEFROST AND SERVE: Cook stems from frozen in boiling salted

water for 3-7 minutes, depending upon thickness.
USES: As a vegetable accompaniment. Serve tossed in butter, lemon juice and black pepper, or coat in a cheese sauce if you like.

CAPONS

See *Chickens* (page 62)

CARAMEL

Caramel can be frozen either in small pieces, crushed or as a sauce. Place in a rigid container. Seal, label and freeze.

STORAGE TIME: Up to 12 months.

TO DEFROST AND SERVE: Defrost at room temperature for 1-2 hours.

USES: As a decoration, flavouring agent, for adding to ice cream mixtures and as a sauce for serving with puddings and desserts.

CARP

Carp is a large fresh-water fish found in slow running waters. These fish can grow to over 15 kg/33 lbs. As they inhabit muddy waters they have an earthy flavour to them.

SELECTING FOR FREEZING
Choose fish that is really fresh, ideally within 12-24 hours of the catch. Fresh fish can be recognised by its firm flesh, clear, full and shiny eyes and clean smell. Steaks, cutlets and fillets should have firm, closely packed flakes; any with a watery or fibrous appearance are stale.

PREPARATION FOR FREEZING
Wash, clean and gut carefully, scraping off the scales. Fillet larger fish but leave smaller fish whole. Remove head and wash in water to which a little vinegar and salt has been added. Pat dry with absorbent kitchen paper.

TO FREEZE
Wrap individual whole fish in cling film, then overwrap in polythene bags. Exclude as much air as possible and seal. Interleave steaks and fillets, then pack together in bags. Seal, label and freeze.

STORAGE TIME: Up to 3 months.

TO DEFROST AND SERVE: Thaw whole fish in wrappings in the refrigerator overnight or for 4-6 hours then cook as fresh. Cook steaks and fillets from frozen as for commercially frozen fish.

USES: Stuff and bake whole fish. Fillets may be grilled, fried or baked.

CARROTS

It is only really worth freezing young spring carrots, available from April onwards. Prepare as soon after picking or purchase as possible.

SELECTING FOR FREEZING
Look for bunches with bright green tops and carrots that are even-sized. Those with smooth skins that are no thicker than a man's finger are perfect.

PREPARATION FOR FREEZING
Slice the tops off, then wash thoroughly under cold running water. Scrub rather than peel.

TO FREEZE
Grade according to size and freeze whole or slice or dice larger ones.
Pack whole carrots straight into polythene bags for short-term storage of up to 6 months or blanch if you intend to keep them longer. Blanch in boiling water for 3 minutes, drain, cool in iced water, drain again and pat dry with absorbent kitchen paper. Pack in usable quantities in polythene bags or open freeze on trays until solid, then pack in bags, seal, label and freeze or return to the freezer. Diced or sliced carrots should be blanched as above for 2 minutes. Open freeze on trays until solid. Pack in usable quantities in polythene bags, seal, label and return to the freezer.

STORAGE TIME: Unblanched whole and diced or sliced carrots up to 6 months; blanched whole and diced or sliced carrots up to 12 months.

TO DEFROST AND SERVE: Cook whole, sliced or diced carrots from frozen in boiling salted water for 4-6 minutes, depending upon size.

USES: Whole, sliced or diced carrots can be served as a vegetable accompaniment with butter and seasonings. Sliced or diced carrots can be added to casseroles, stews and stir-fry mixtures and also used to make carrot-based soups.

CASSEROLES

Most casserole recipes freeze well and no special freezer recipe is needed. It is a useful and cheap way to use your casserole serving dish as a mould for making your own foil container.

Line the clean casserole with foil, leaving plenty above the sides to fold over. Fill with the cooked dish and freeze until firm enough to remove the food in foil mould from the dish. The dish, of course, is then back available for normal kitchen use. Wrap the now solid casserole firmly with additional foil or in a polythene bag, seal, label and return to the freezer.

For reheating, peel away the foil from the frozen casserole and place back in the ovenproof serving dish, where you know it will be a perfect fit. Polythene bags can also be used as a mould for such dishes and can be stripped away for reheating.

STORAGE TIME: Storage time will be dependent upon the ingredients used but can be up to 3 months.

TO DEFROST AND SERVE: Again there are no hard and fast rules, times and procedures will depend upon the ingredients and quantities frozen. A typical quantity of beef casserole, to serve 4, should be left to stand at room temperature for 2½ hours, then reheated for about 30 minutes.

CAULIFLOWERS

Whether you choose to freeze winter or summer cauliflowers the procedure is the same.

SELECTING FOR FREEZING
Only choose really fresh cauliflowers that are white and firm with no signs of 'blowing' or 'feathering' of the curds for freezing. The surrounding leaves should be crisp and bright green.

PREPARATION FOR FREEZING
Break or cut the curds into florets each about 5 cm/2 inches in diameter. Wash well and grade according to size.

TO FREEZE
Blanch in boiling water to which 15 ml/1 tablespoon lemon juice has been added. Allow 2-3 minutes depending upon size. Drain, cool in iced water, drain again and pat dry with absorbent kitchen paper. Open freeze on trays until solid, pack in usable quantities in polythene bags, seal, label and return to the freezer.

STORAGE TIME: Up to 6 months.

TO DEFROST AND SERVE: Cook from frozen in boiling salted water for 4-6 minutes, depending upon size.

USES: Serve as a vegetable accompaniment with butter and seasonings, or coated with a cheese or béchamel sauce. Use to make soups, vegetable mixtures and stir-fries.

CAVIAR

If you are fortunate enough to have some of the world's greatest delicacies left over, then don't be tempted to freeze it. The exquisite flavour and unusual texture will be ruined. So go on, spoil yourself and guzzle the remainder!

CELERIAC

This globe-shaped root vegetable looks rather like a knobbly turnip but tastes like celery and freezes well.

SELECTING FOR FREEZING
Choose firm, small roots. Avoid those that are very knobbly since they will take a long time to prepare. Reject any with any signs of disease or rotting.

PREPARATION FOR FREEZING
Peel and wash, then cut into cubes or thick slices, or grate.

TO FREEZE
Blanch cubes and slices in boiling water for 1-2 minutes, depending upon size. Drain, cool in iced water, drain again and pat dry with absorbent kitchen paper. Open freeze on trays until solid, then pack in usable quantities in polythene bags. Seal, label and return to the freezer.
  Grated celeriac should be blanched in boiling water for 1 minute. Drain, cool in iced water, drain again and pat dry with absorbent kitchen paper. Pack in polythene bags or rigid containers. Seal, label and freeze.

STORAGE TIME: Up to 12 months.

TO DEFROST AND SERVE: Cook cubes and slices from frozen in boiling salted water for about 5 minutes until tender. Use grated celeriac from frozen. Add to boiling salted water for 3 minutes or add straight to casseroles and soups from frozen.

USES: Use cubed and sliced celeriac as a vegetable accompaniment with butter and seasonings. It is also very good with a béchamel, parsley or Hollandaise sauce. It can also be used with other vegetables to make a stir-fry mixture. Grated celeriac can be added to soups and casseroles.

CELERY

Although celery cannot be eaten raw after freezing, it is well worth storing in the freezer for serving as a vegetable accompaniment or as a made-up dish.

SELECTING FOR FREEZING
Select large, firm heads with no sign of ageing on the outer stalks. The stems should have wide, fat bases, while the leaves should be crisp and green.

PREPARATION FOR FREEZING
Cut off the base with a sharp knife and separate the stems. Trim off the leaves (and use in salads or as a garnish if you like), then wash the stems thoroughly. Scrub or scrape with a small knife if necessary. Cut the stems into 5 cm/2 inch lengths.

TO FREEZE
Blanch in boiling water for 3 minutes. Drain, cool in iced water, drain again and pat dry with absorbent kitchen paper. Pack in usable quantities in polythene bags. Seal, label and freeze.

STORAGE TIME: Up to 9 months.

TO DEFROST AND SERVE: Cook celery from frozen in boiling salted water for about 10 minutes until tender. Also use from frozen in soups, casseroles and stews. Alternatively it can be defrosted in its wrappings at room temperature for about 2 hours and then used as a vegetable in a stir-fry dish.

USES: As a vegetable accompaniment tossed in butter and seasonings or coated with a tomato, béchamel or cheese sauce. It can also be used in gratins, soups, casseroles, stews and in stir-fry mixtures.

CHEESE

Hard, soft, blue and cream cheese all freeze successfully and take up little space in the freezer. Since they are a staple food and invariably useful, especially if ready grated, they are worthy of freezing.

PREPARATION FOR FREEZING AND TO FREEZE

HARD CHEESE:(such as Cheddar, Cheshire and Edam) should be frozen cut into 225 g/8 oz blocks. Wrap in foil or cling film, then overwrap in a polythene bag. For grated hard cheese, grate in the usual way then pack in usable quantities in polythene bags. Seal, label and freeze.
SOFT CHEESE: (such as Brie, Camembert and Mozzarella). Freeze only mature soft cheese – cut into usable quantities. Wrap in foil or cling film, then overwrap in a polythene bag. Seal, label and freeze.

CREAM CHEESE: Spoon cream cheese in usable quantities into rigid containers. Seal, label and freeze.
Follow the instructions above for blue cheese depending upon whether it is a hard or soft blue cheese.

STORAGE TIME: 3-6 months depending upon freshness.

TO DEFROST AND SERVE: Thaw hard and cream cheeses in their wrappings in the refrigerator overnight. Whisk cream cheese to get rid of any granular appearance before serving.
Defrost soft cheeses for 24 hours in the refrigerator, then 24 hours at room temperature. Use grated cheese from frozen. Use all cheeses soon after defrosting.

CHEESECAKES

All cheesecakes freeze well, ie baked and unbaked, with and without topping, and with varying ingredients.
Open freeze to prevent damage, until solid, pack in foil or a polythene bag with cardboard support to prevent damage or a rigid container. Storage time is 1-2 months. Defrost in the refrigerator overnight.

CHERRIES

Cherries freeze well and since their season is a short one they merit some freezer space for enjoyment the rest of the year.

SELECTING FOR FREEZING

Look out for cherries in June and July, although some may be on sale as early as late May in a good year. Choose red or black cherries that are firm, with a good glossy skin and plump flesh. Avoid those with signs of split skins or marking due to disease.

PREPARATION FOR FREEZING

Cherries can be frozen whole or poached. To prepare whole cherries, remove the stalks, wash well then leave to soak in iced water for about 20-30 minutes to plump the flesh. Dry with absorbent kitchen paper. Stone with a cherry stoner or halve and remove the stones by hand. Poach whole cherries, without their stones, in a little water until tender with sugar to taste. Allow to cool.

TO FREEZE

Whole uncooked cherries can be frozen as a free-flow pack, a dry sugar pack or as a sugar syrup pack.

Free-flow packs are only suitable for those cherries that are very sweet. Open freeze on trays until solid, then pack into polythene bags. Seal, label and return to the freezer.

A dry-sugar pack is best for sweet red cherries that are ideal for pie and crumble making. Pack such cherries in usable quantities in rigid containers, sprinkling each layer with sugar and allowing 225 g/8 oz sugar for every 450 g/1 lb fruit. Seal, label and freeze.

A sugar syrup pack is suitable for sweet and sour cherries. Pack in usable quantities in rigid containers. Sweet cherries should be covered with a medium sugar syrup (see page 25), adding 45 ml/3 tablespoons lemon juice to prevent discolouration; and sour cherries with a heavy sugar syrup (see page 25), again adding 45 ml/3 tablespoons lemon juice to prevent discolouration. Leave a 2 cm/¾ inch headspace. Cover, label and freeze.

Poached cherries should be spooned into rigid containers in usable quantities, leaving a 2 cm/¾ inch headspace. Seal, label and freeze.

STORAGE TIME: Whole uncooked cherries up to 12 months; poached cherries up to 8 months.

TO DEFROST AND SERVE: Leave all types of uncooked cherries to defrost at room temperature for about 3 hours, then use immediately to prevent discolouration.

Defrost poached cherries in their containers for 3 hours to serve cold or reheat gently over a very low heat, stirring occasionally, to serve warm or hot.

USES: Use in pies, puddings, preserves, jam making, flans, fruit salads, ice creams, sauces and crumbles: the poached fruit can be puréed to make a sauce for puddings and desserts or for flavouring ice creams, whips and mousses.

CHESTNUTS

Sweet chestnuts, available in the autumn and winter, contain a low proportion of fat so are suitable for freezing. Sweet chestnuts are best frozen skinned and whole, or as an unsweetened purée.

SELECTING FOR FREEZING

Choose large plump chestnuts with glossy skins that show no signs of splitting, damage or disease.

PREPARATION FOR FREEZING

Wash and make a small slit just through the skin of each one. Place in a pan, cover with water and bring to the boil. Remove from the pan with a slotted spoon, a few at a time and skin with a small sharp knife as quickly as possible. Do not allow to cool or the skin adheres to the flesh and the task becomes virtually impossible. Whole chestnuts need to further preparation.

If you wish to make a purée then place the chestnuts in a blender or food processor and purée until smooth.

TO FREEZE

Pack whole nuts in usable quantities in rigid containers. Seal, label and freeze.

Chestnut purée should be spooned into rigid containers in usable quantities, leaving a 2 cm/¾ inch headspace. Seal, label and freeze.

STORAGE TIME: Up to 6 months.

TO DEFROST AND SERVE: Leave whole chestnuts to stand in their container at room temperature until they can be separated. Cook as for fresh.

Chestnut purée should be left to stand in its container at room temperature until it can be beaten with a fork to use, about 2 hours.

USES: Steam or boil whole chestnuts to serve with vegetables; Brussels Sprouts with chestnuts are a firm and traditional favourite. Use in casseroles and soups too. Chestnut purée can be used in savoury stuffings, or sweetened and used to make desserts.

CHICKENS

It has become much easier to buy fresh chicken for the home freezer and, since chicken often features on the family menu, it is worth freezing a few to cope with emergencies or when prices and quality merit the purchase. Farm-bred rather than battery-bred are the obvious choice but also consider special types like corn-fed chickens for special recipes and occasions. Consider too baby chickens (poussins) for freezing, they are competitively priced and, depending upon size, will feed 1-2 people. Likewise capons, larger than roasting chickens, depending upon size, can feed up to 6 people.

—— RAW CHICKENS ——
SELECTING FOR FREEZING

Choose young plump birds. The recommended sizes for home freezing are:

Baby chicken (poussins) 700-1000g/1½-2 lbs
Young chickens 1.1-1.6 kg/2½-3½ lbs
Capons 2.3-3.2 kg/5-7 lbs

It should be borne in mind that the larger the chicken, the higher the flesh-to-bone ratio, therefore bigger birds are often better value for money. Select fleshy birds with a light layering of fat under the skin, with the skin untorn and not blemished in any way.

PREPARATION FOR FREEZING

Pluck and hang if necessary. Singe small remaining feathers and hairs over a flame. Remove head and feet, and draw the entrails, separating the giblets (which should be frozen separately from the chicken if a long storage life is desired). Chill thoroughly in the refrigerator before freezing. Many farms, butchers and poultry suppliers will prepare chickens up to this stage for you if you like.

TO FREEZE

Whole birds should be prepared as for cooking with legs and wings well trussed to the body to give a compact shape. Place a small pad of foil over any protruding bones so that they do not puncture the packaging. Wrap in a gusseted polythene bag taking care to mould around the chicken removing as much air as possible. Seal, label and freeze. **NB** It is not advisable to stuff chicken before freezing because the stuffing itself takes a long time to reach the desired low temperature, thus giving possible food spoilage organisms the time and warm conditions necessary for their growth. The storage time in the freezer would also then be reduced to that of the stuffing (little over a month) making unstuffed chicken a much more desirable freezer product. Pack giblets in a rigid container. Seal, label and freeze.

STORAGE TIME: Up to 12 months for whole chicken; 3 months for giblets.

TO DEFROST AND SERVE: ALL CHICKENS MUST BE COMPLETELY DEFROSTED BEFORE COOKING. Defrost at room temperature or in the refrigerator for the times below:

WEIGHT	AT ROOM TEMP	IN REFRIGERATOR
1 kg/2 lb	8 hours	28 hours
1.4 kg/3 lb	9 hours	32 hours
1.8 kg/4 lb	10 hours	38 hours
2.3 kg/5 lb	12 hours	44 hours
2.7 kg/6 lb	14 hours	50 hours

Giblets should be defrosted in their container in the refrigerator for about 12 hours.

USES: Chickens are a good low-fat choice (especially if cooked or served without the skin) for main meal eating. They can be roasted, grilled, sautéed, barbecued, fried, boiled, braised, steamed, casseroled and stir-fried, which makes them a most versatile meat. Giblets can be used to make stock, soups, pâtés and sautéed to make a light main meal.

CHICKEN PORTIONS

Chicken portions, be they halves, quarters, drumsticks, thighs, wings, breasts or chopped chicken meat, should be prepared for the freezer like whole birds. Either pack separately, or pack together separating each portion with interleaving paper for easy removal when required. Seal, label and freeze. Defrost completely before cooking as above.

STORAGE TIME: Up to 12 months.

USES: Portions can be roasted, fried, grilled, sautéed, barbecued, casseroled, braised and stir-fried to make countless dishes suitable for starter and main course serving.

COOKED CHICKEN MEAT

Whole chickens and chicken portions may be cooked and frozen on or off the bone and are useful for salads, picnic and packed lunch fare, party food and for making many composite dishes where cooked chicken is required. Slices of chicken are often best coated in a sauce or gravy for long term storage so that very little drying out takes place.
NB Chicken that has been frozen once in its cooked state should never be defrosted and then refrozen.

STORAGE TIME: Cooked whole chickens up to 2 months; casseroled or in a sauce or gravy up to 2 months; and slices, if not coated in a sauce or gravy, up to 1 month.

CHICORY

This vegetable most confusingly is also known in some countries as endive. It can be used raw or cooked but because its texture changes appreciably during freezing, only chicory for cooked use should be frozen.

SELECTING FOR FREEZING

Choose heads that have a regular conical shape and tightly packed leaves. The leaves should be crisp and white topped with green.

PREPARATION FOR FREEZING

Trim the bases with a sharp knife (use stainless steel to prevent discolouration), then wipe clean and remove any below-par outside leaves.

TO FREEZE

Blanch heads in boiling water for 4 minutes. Drain, cool quickly in iced water, drain again and pat dry with absorbent kitchen paper. Pack in usable quantities in rigid containers or polythene bags. Seal, label and freeze.

STORAGE TIME: Up to 5 months.

TO DEFROST AND SERVE: Cook heads from frozen in boiling salted water for about 8 minutes until tender. Alternatively braise from frozen in a well-flavoured stock. Or defrost chicory in its wrappings at room temperature for 2 hours, then squeeze to remove excess water and use as required.

USES: As a vegetable accompaniment, boiled and served with a cheese or béchamel sauce. Braised in stock and dusted with a little Parmesan cheese as a delicious accompaniment to Italian dishes.

CHILLIES

Chillies, which look like slimline peppers, are the fiery hot cousins of sweet peppers. They dry superbly but since they take up little freezer space, a few prepared in the freezer can be useful.

SELECTING FOR FREEZING

Choose smooth shiny chillies that do not show the slightest signs of wrinkling.

PREPARATION FOR FREEZING

It is advisable to wear rubber gloves for this procedure. Cut the chillies in half and remove the stalks, woody bases, seeds and any membrane. Dice or cut into strips as you like. Do not touch your nose, eyes or mouth during this time as the juices from the chillies will sting very badly.

TO FREEZE

Open freeze on trays until solid, then pack in polythene bags. Seal, label and freeze. This will give you a free-flow pack.

STORAGE TIME: Up to 12 months.

TO DEFROST AND SERVE: Use from frozen by simply adding to the dishes you are cooking. Alternatively, defrost in their wrappings at room temperature for 1-2 hours.

USES: Use judiciously in curries and other spicy cooked dishes, in sauces, salads and salsas.

CHIPS

These are an excellent product to come from the freezer but simply not worth all the trouble of preparation, when commercially prepared ones are available with such good quality. If desired however, blanch chipped potatoes in hot oil for 2 minutes. Drain thoroughly on absorbent kitchen paper and open freeze until solid. Pack in polythene bags, seal, label and return to the freezer. Storage time for home-made chips is up to 3 months.

CHOCOLATE

Chocolate is used in many recipes, ie cakes, gâteaux, sponges, icings, soufflés, chocolate buttercream, chocolate sauce etc and freezes extremely well.

Chocolate decorations also freeze well and are handy to have available in the freezer. Chocolate caraque, grated chocolate, chocolate curls, chocolate leaves, chocolate squares and shapes can all be frozen successfully.

TO FREEZE

Delicate decorations should be packed in rigid containers, interleaving where necessary. Seal, label and freeze.

STORAGE TIME: Up to 2 months.

TO DEFROST AND SERVE: Remove from the freezer and in most cases, position or sprinkle on the cake or dessert while still frozen. Leave to defrost in the refrigerator or at room temperature depending upon end use. A slight bloom may be found upon thawing, as with chocolate icing, but this does not affect the flavour.

CLEMENTINES

Regarded by many as a practically seedless variety of tangerine, and by others as a cross between the tangerine and sweet orange, the clementine is mainly grown in North African countries, Italy, Spain and Israel and exported to this country just before and just after Christmas. It has a wonderful sweet flavour and is worth freezing because its season is so short. The orangey-red, easily removed skin also makes this possible in a trice.

SELECTING FOR FREEZING

Buy shiny, firm fruit with plump, never dry or shrivelled-looking skins. Choose specimens that weigh heavy for their size – it is a sure sign that they are juicy not dry or pithy.

PREPARATION FOR FREEZING

Peel, then separate into segments, removing any excess pith and any visible pips if necessary.

TO FREEZE

Pack in usable quantities in rigid containers, sprinkling between each layer with sugar to taste. Alternatively, cover the segments with a medium sugar syrup (made from 350 g/12 oz sugar to 600 ml/1 pint water). Seal, label and freeze.

STORAGE TIME: Freeze for up to 12 months.

TO DEFROST AND SERVE: Defrost frozen clementine segments in their container for about 2 hours at room temperature.

USES: Use in fruit salads, breakfast citrus dishes or fruit-based desserts.

COCKLES

Cockles with their pale shells are widely available in the Mediterranean, Baltic and American Atlantic. They can be eaten raw or cooked. It isn't always easy to find fresh cockles for freezing, but if you do they are worthy of a little freezer space.

For freezing follow the instructions for freezing MUSSELS (see page 114).

COCONUT

Coconuts are imported in the winter months and are well worth freezing for use in cooking because the flavour of fresh coconut is far superior to that of dried.

SELECTING FOR FREEZING
When choosing coconuts, hold the fruit in your hand, it should weigh heavy. Shake it and listen for the sound of the milk - this is a good indication that the coconut is fresh.

PREPARATION FOR FREEZING
Pierce a few eyes in the shell with a skewer then pour off the liquid inside. Place the shell on a heavy surface or the floor and hit several times with a hammer until it cracks into pieces. Scrape away the flesh from the shell then grate or shred using a grater or food processor.

TO FREEZE
Open freeze until solid, then pack in polythene bags. Seal, label and return to the freezer.

STORAGE TIME: Up to 6 months.

TO DEFROST AND SERVE: Tip whole packs or large quantities of frozen coconut into a colander and leave at room temperature to defrost for 2 hours, then use as fresh. Small amounts of coconut sprinkled over food will defrost in just a few minutes.

USES: Fresh coconut is particularly useful in Indian and oriental dishes, especially for mellowing fiery hot curry dishes. The milk, obtained by soaking grated coconut flesh in water, is a staple ingredient in Indonesian and Thai cooking. Also use to make cakes, biscuits, curries and desserts.

COD

Cod is a deep-sea fish available all year round but best from October to March. More cod than any other fish reaches British ports. It can be bought whole, in steaks or in fillets and lends itself to many ways of cooking. Fillets of cod are also sold smoked.

SELECTING FOR FREEZING
Fresh cod can be recognised by its firm flesh, clear, full and shiny eyes, bright red gills and clean smell. Steaks, cutlets and fillets should have firm, closely packed flakes; any with a fibrous or watery appearance are stale. Fish with flesh that has a blue or green tinge is almost certainly not

fresh - on flat fish, this is most apparent on the dark side. Buy from a reputable supplier and check that the fish has not already been frozen previously.

PREPARATION FOR FREEZING

Prepare within 24 hours of the catch. Gut and clean, remove scales and fins. Cut off heads and tails and remove the skin if you like. Leave whole if small, cut into steaks or fillets if large. Rinse under cold running water and pat dry with absorbent kitchen paper.

TO FREEZE

Wrap individual whole fish in cling film, then overwrap in polythene bags. Exclude as much air as possible. Seal, label and freeze.

Interleave steaks and fillets, then pack together in polythene bags. Exclude as much air as possible. Seal, label and freeze.

STORAGE TIME: Up to 3 months.

TO DEFROST AND SERVE: Defrost whole fish in its wrappings in the refrigerator overnight, or for 3-4 hours at room temperature, then cook as fresh. Cook steaks and fillets from frozen as for commercially frozen fish. Allow about one-third to one-half extra cooking time, graduating from low to high heat.

USES: Cod can be steamed, boiled, grilled, baked, fried, barbecued, casseroled and poached for countless starter, main course and snack or light meal offerings.

COFFEE

SELECTING FOR FREEZING

Coffee is excellent for freezing as a flavouring for cooking or simply for drinking.

PREPARATION FOR FREEZING

To use as a flavouring for cooking, make up the coffee as normal, using a strong concentration of coffee. Cool and freeze in ice cube trays. When frozen put the cubes in a polythene bag with a squirt of soda water, seal, label and return to the freezer.

To freeze fresh coffee, extract as much air as possible from the bags, label, seal and freeze. Since coffee deteriorates after roasting ensure that your supply is absolutely fresh.

STORAGE TIME: Freeze coffee cubes for up to 3 months. Ground

❄ coffee and fresh coffee beans can be frozen for up to 12 months.

USES: For drinking but also for flavouring cake and pudding mixtures, frostings and icings, ice creams and mousses and other coffee-based recipes.

COLEY

Also known as coal-fish or saithe, this is a fish of the cod family. It takes its name from its black skin and is found in the North Sea. It is available from September to February. Prepare and cook like cod.

For freezing follow the instructions for freezing COD (see page 69).

COMMERCIALLY FROZEN FOODS

These are foods that have been prepared and frozen by the manufacturer using high levels of technology not easily imitated at home. This is why some products seem better frozen commercially, peas for example. Methods used for freezing include blast freezing, plate freezing and cryogenic freezing.

In a food freezer, operating at -18°C/0°F, bought frozen foods can usually be stored for up to 3 months but always check the packaging for specific manufacturer's instructions relating to sell-buy and use-by dates.

COOKIES

See *Biscuits* (page 41)

COTTAGE CHEESE

Cottage cheese does tend to have a granular appearance after defrosting and so is not the best cheese to freeze. This appearance can however be improved by adding a little cream before using the defrosted cheese if you like. Freeze only really fresh cottage cheese. Pack into usable quantities and freeze for 2-3 months. Defrost in the refrigerator overnight and then allow to come to room temperature before serving and eating.

COURGETTES

Courgettes are like miniature marrows and as such are vegetables with a high water content. Their use in the freezer is therefore limited although they can be used to make ratatouille which freezes superbly.

SELECTING FOR FREEZING

Undoubtedly the best courgettes for the freezer are those that are firm and young that generally appear at the beginning of the season. These small, very young courgettes have the best flavour and the lowest water content. Check that skins are firm and shiny and free from blemishes.

PREPARATION FOR FREEZING

Wipe or wash if necessary then trim the ends but do not peel. They can be frozen whole or cut in half lengthways. Larger courgettes are better cut into slices or chunks. The courgettes can also be cooked and frozen as a purée.

TO FREEZE

Whole, halved, sliced and chunks of courgettes should be blanched in boiling water for 2 minutes. Drain and cool in iced water, drain again and pat dry with absorbent kitchen paper. Pack in usable quantities in polythene bags, seal, label and freeze.

Courgette purée should be spooned into rigid containers, leaving a 2 cm/¾ inch headspace. Seal, label and freeze.

STORAGE TIME: Whole, halved, sliced and chunks of courgette for up to 9 months; courgette purée for up to 6 months.

TO DEFROST AND SERVE: Whole, halved, sliced and chunks of courgette should be allowed to defrost in their wrappings at room temperature for about 2 hours. Courgette purée should be allowed to defrost in its container at room temperature for 2 hours. Reheat courgette purée over a low heat with a knob of butter and seasonings.

USES: Serve as a vegetable accompaniment sautéed in butter with seasonings and herbs if you like; coat in a batter and deep fry for a vegetable side dish; add to casseroles near the end of the cooking time; use as an ingredient for ratatouille or a savoury mixture to layer between pasta; add to savoury stuffings; or stuff halves and bake, sprinkled with cheese. Courgette purée can be served as a vegetable accompaniment or used in a vegetable terrine if well flavoured with seasonings or herbs.

CRAB

Crab must be absolutely fresh, as well as being freshly boiled and cooled before freezing.

SELECTING FOR FREEZING

Choose fresh or cooked crabs that feel heavy for their size with a good clean smell. Shake them lightly, there should be no sound of water inside. Crab is available all year round but at its best from May to October.

PREPARATION FOR FREEZING

Boil and cool in the usual way.

TO FREEZE

For best results closely wrap the whole crab in heavy gauge polythene or foil. Alternatively, remove the cooked crab meat from the shell and pack the white and brown meat in separate small containers, or arrange meats as for serving in a well-scrubbed crab shell. Cover with cling film and overwrap closely with polythene. Seal, label and freeze.

STORAGE TIME: Up to 1 month.

TO DEFROST AND SERVE: Defrost in the wrappings in the refrigerator for 6-8 hours, then eat or use as fresh.

USES: Crab can be baked, steamed or boiled. It makes a delicious sandwich filling and is probably best appreciated in its simplest form, boiled, and served with brown bread and butter.

CRANBERRIES

Cranberries retain their colour, flavour and texture in the freezer and are well worth freezing because their season in the shops and markets is extremely brief.

SELECTING FOR FREEZING

Look out for bright red, shiny berries that show no signs of mould. Usually available in November and December, buy them as soon as you see them since they disappear fast.

PREPARATION FOR FREEZING

Wash and pick over so that any dry or shrivelled berries are removed and discarded.

TO FREEZE

Cranberries can be frozen as whole berries or as a sauce. Whole berries should be placed on trays in the freezer and frozen until solid. The berries should then be packed, in usable quantities, into polythene bags, sealed, labelled and returned to the freezer.

Cranberry sauce can be made by cooking whole cranberries in water and sugar (allow 450 ml/¾ pint water and 450 g/1 lb sugar to every 450 g/1 lb cranberries). Boil until the cranberry skins pop, boil for a further 5 minutes, then cool quickly. Spoon into rigid containers, in usable quantities, leaving a 2 cm/¾ inch headspace. Seal, label and freeze.

STORAGE TIME: Up to 12 months.

TO DEFROST AND SERVE: Leave whole cranberries to stand in their wrappings at room temperature for 2 hours or reheat from frozen.

Defrost cranberry sauce at room temperature for 2 hours. If you wish to serve the sauce hot then reheat over a low heat, stirring frequently and adding a little extra water if the sauce starts to stick.

USES: Use cranberries in sauces, jams, jellies, desserts and stuffings. Cranberry sauce can be used in cake making, mousses, sorbets, ice creams and other desserts.

CREAM

Only cream containing more than 35% butterfat will freeze successfully – this means that only double cream, whipping cream and clotted cream will freeze well. Single cream (with 18% butterfat) and soured cream (with less than 35% butterfat) will separate when defrosted. Commercially prepared frozen single cream is available but it is not possible to imitate this freezing process domestically.

DOUBLE CREAM

Freeze only very fresh double cream. To overcome any tendency to separate on defrosting, the cream should be partially whipped or slightly sweetened by adding 5 ml/1 teaspoon sugar to 150 ml/¼ pint double cream. Pack in a rigid container, leaving 2 cm/¾ inch headspace. A good idea is to freeze some cream in ice cube trays, as this gives approximately one cube to 15 ml/1 tablespoon cream. If the cream is whipped so that it holds its shape it can also be frozen as piped decorations. Pipe onto a tray and freeze until solid. Lift with a palette knife into a rigid container, seal, label and freeze.

STORAGE TIME: 3-4 months.

TO DEFROST AND SERVE: Allow to defrost slowly in the refrigerator for several hours or overnight. Use as for fresh cream. Place frozen piped decorations in position on the dish and allow to defrost for 1-2 hours.

CLOTTED CREAM

Freeze only really fresh clotted cream. Leave in the retail pack and seal with freezer tape or store in a rigid container, seal, label and freeze.

STORAGE TIME: Up to 12 months.

TO DEFROST AND SERVE: Allow to defrost slowly in the refrigerator for several hours or overnight. Use as for fresh clotted cream.

WHIPPING CREAM

Freeze only really fresh whipping cream. Partially whip the cream or stir in a little sugar, allowing 5 ml/1 teaspoon to every 150 ml/¼ pint cream to overcome any tendency to separate on thawing. Whip totally if preferred and pipe rosettes onto trays for decorations. Open freeze until solid, lift with a palette knife into a rigid box, seal, label and freeze.

STORAGE TIME: Up to 2 months.

TO DEFROST AND SERVE: Defrost in the refrigerator overnight. Use as for fresh whipping cream. Place frozen piped decorations into position on the dish and allow to defrost for 1-2 hours.

CROISSANTS

Baked croissants freeze well. The unbaked dough can also be frozen in bulk, and may be stored for up to 4 weeks. Prepare up to, but not including, the final rolling.

BAKED
PREPARATION AND FREEZING

Pack in a single layer in a polythene bag or place on a foil tray and seal with foil. Seal, label and freeze.

STORAGE TIME: Up to 3 months.

TO DEFROST AND SERVE: Place frozen croissants, wrapped in foil, in a moderately hot oven (200°C/400°F/Gas 6) for 15 minutes, or leave in their wrappings at room temperature for 1½-2 hours, then refresh and warm through, still wrapped in foil, in a hot oven (220°C/425°F/Gas 7) for 5 minutes.

USES: Serve with butter and preserves, or use to make a savoury snack filled with ham and cheese.

CROÛTONS

SELECTING FOR FREEZING

Croûtons and small fried bread shapes freeze well and can be prepared in quantity. When frozen they remain separate and the required quantity can be easily removed.

TO FREEZE

Pack in polythene bags, a sealed polythene container or self-seal bags for easy access. Seal, label and freeze.

STORAGE TIME: Freeze for up to 1 month.

TO DEFROST AND SERVE: Place frozen, uncovered larger-sized croûtons in a moderately hot oven (200°C, 400°F, Gas Mark 6) for 5 minutes. Tiny croûtons for soups can be added straight into hot soups.

USES: Use croûtons and fried bread shapes for canapés and party snacks and for adding to soups and salads.

CUCUMBERS

Cucumbers are not suitable for freezing for usual use in salads, however, they can be puréed and used to make a soup or sauce.

SELECTING FOR FREEZING

For reasons of economy buy cucumbers in July and August when the crop is at its peak. Select good firm specimens but don't worry too much about their shape – indeed look out for mis-shapen bargains.

PREPARATION FOR FREEZING

Peel, chop and work to a purée in a food processor or blender.

TO FREEZE

Pour, in usable quantities, into rigid containers, leaving a 2 cm/¾ inch headspace. Seal, label and freeze.

STORAGE TIME: Up to 2 months.

TO DEFROST AND SERVE: Defrost in the container at room temperature for several hours, then use hot or cold in soups and sauces.

CURRANTS, BLACK, RED AND WHITE

Black, red and white currants all freeze well and are worthy of some freezer space since they prove endlessly versatile in many recipes.

SELECTING FOR FREEZING

Choose firm, plump, perfectly ripe fruit. Avoid any that are under-ripe, wrinkled or showing any signs of damage. Look out for fruit in late June through to early August.

PREPARATION FOR FREEZING

Separate the currants from their stems. Prepare either as whole currants, stewed currants, currant purée or currant juice.

There is no need to blanch whole currants unless you wish to use them at a later date for jams. If you do then blanch for 1 minute, drain, cool in iced water, drain again and pat dry on absorbent kitchen paper.

For stewed currants, cook in the minimum amount of water with sugar to taste. Allow to cool.

For currant purée, cook as above then pass through a fine nylon sieve, or purée in a blender or food processor then sieve to remove any pips.

For currant juice, (only really suitable for blackcurrants) stew in enough water to cover, sieve or purée in a blender or food processor then strain through muslin to give a clear juice.

TO FREEZE

Whole currants can be frozen free-flow. Open freeze on trays until solid, then pack into polythene bags, seal, label and return to the freezer.

To freeze whole currants in a dry sugar pack, pack the currants in usable quantities in rigid containers, sprinkling sugar between each layer and allowing 100-175 g/4-6 oz sugar for every 450 g/1 lb fruit, according to taste. Seal, label and freeze.

To freeze whole currants in a sugar syrup pack, pack in usable quantities in rigid containers and cover with a medium sugar syrup (see page 25). Leave a 2 cm/¾ inch headspace. Seal, label and freeze.

Currant purée should be spooned into rigid containers in usable quantities, leaving a 2 cm/¾ inch headspace. Seal, label and freeze.

Currant juice should be frozen as for currant purée.

STORAGE TIME: Free-flow, dry sugar pack and sugar syrup packs for up to 12 months; currant purée up to 8 months; and currant juice for up to 12 months.

TO DEFROST AND SERVE: Free-flow, dry sugar and sugar syrup

packs can be cooked from frozen in pies, puddings and cooked recipes. To defrost and use uncooked, leave to stand in their wrappings at room temperature for about 45 minutes.

Stewed currants should be defrosted in their container at room temperature for 1-2 hours. Alternatively, heat from frozen over a very low heat, stirring frequently.

Currant purée and currant juice should be defrosted in its container at room temperature for 1-2 hours.

USES: Use whole currants in pies, puddings, fruit salads, cheesecakes, summer puddings, jams, jellies and as an accompaniment to rich meats and game. Stewed currants can be used in puddings and pies or as simple dessert for serving with custard or cream. Use currant purée for ice creams, sorbets, mousses and sauces. Currant juice makes a wonderful refreshing drink but can also be used to make ice lollipops for children.

CURRIES

Since most curries taste better when reheated to serve a day after making, they lend themselves well to freezer storage.

Curries made with freshly-ground spices mellow slightly during storage; those made with curry powder lose a little piquancy after a couple of months. The true flavour of the spices tends to taste 'peppery' after 3-4 months storage and the salt tends to intensify. For these reasons a storage time of up to 2 months is recommended. Make sure of adequate packaging and good sealing to avoid flavour transfer in the freezer.

CUSTARD

Frozen custard is not very satisfactory, because of its high milk content. It tends to separate on defrosting and lose its smooth appearance. This will be a problem when making trifle, but a good alternative is canned custard, which is homogenised, and although it does not set as well as home-made, if the ingredients are slightly less moist, it is most acceptable.

It is not recommended that egg custard should be frozen on its own or in a pie, as it also tends to separate and curdle when thawed. Sometimes it is successful to freeze the raw egg custard, but it is necessary to use more eggs than one might normally use, ie 4 eggs rather than 3 to 600 ml/1 pint milk. Although this can be cooked from frozen, little is gained against preparing fresh.

DANISH PASTRIES

Baked Danish Pastries freeze well. The unbaked dough can also be frozen in bulk.

SELECTING FOR FREEZING

Ideally freeze the pastries without icing so that they can be refreshed in the oven, but they can be frozen when iced.

TO FREEZE

Pack cooled pastries in a polythene bag or rigid container. Seal, label and freeze. Wrap unbaked dough in foil or pack, in usable quantities, in a polythene bag. Seal, label and freeze.

STORAGE TIME: Baked pastries for 3 months, unbaked dough for 6 months.

TO DEFROST AND SERVE: Defrost baked iced pastries in their loosened packaging at room temperature for 1½ hours. Defrost plain pastries as above, then refresh in a moderately hot oven (200°C/ 400°F/ Gas 6) for 5 minutes or bake from frozen at the same temperature for 10 minutes. Leave unbaked dough to defrost in its wrappings in the refrigerator overnight.

DAMSONS

Damsons are a distant relation of the plum but are generally darker in colour, sometimes smaller and invariably tarter in flavour.

SELECTING FOR FREEZING

Select firm, ripe fruit with no sign of splitting skins. Ideally pick or buy and freeze on the same day.

PREPARATION FOR FREEZING

Damsons can be frozen in several ways either as halves or, more successfully, as a purée. Wipe the damsons well or wash if necessary. Halve lengthways and remove the stones. To make a purée, cook halves in the minimum amount of water, with sugar to taste, until tender. Purée in a blender or food processor or pass through a fine nylon sieve.

TO FREEZE

Freeze damson halves dry in sugar or in a syrup. To make a dry sugar pack, pack the damson halves in usable quantities in rigid containers, sprinkling between each layer with sugar. Allow about 225 g/8 oz sugar for each 450 g/1 lb fruit. Seal, label and freeze. Alternatively, pack in rigid containers and cover with a medium sugar syrup, leaving a 2 cm/¾ inch headspace. Seal, label and freeze. Pour damson purée into rigid containers, leaving a 2 cm/¾ inch headspace. Seal, label and freeze.

STORAGE TIME: Up to 12 months.

TO DEFROST AND SERVE: Leave damson halves to stand in their containers at room temperature for about 2 hours then use cold if you like. Alternatively, heat through damsons in a syrup over a low heat until hot and tender. Damson purée should be thawed in its container at room temperature for about 2-3 hours.

USES: Use cold damson halves in fruit salads or with ice creams, mousses or creamed rice. Serve hot with cream or custard or use to make pies and crumbles. Halves can also be used to make jams and jellies. Use the purée as a tart sauce for sweet desserts or cold meats such as pork or game. Serve as a hot sauce for sweet and savoury dishes where its tart flavour is appreciated.

DATES

Fresh dates freeze very well and are worth freezing since they have such a short season in the shops. Christmas time is probably the best time to look out for them and bargains can often be found after the Christmas festivities in January.

SELECTING FOR FREEZING
Look out for plump, moist fruits that look fresh. Reject any dry and shrivelled specimens.

PREPARATION FOR FREEZING
Dates are best frozen without their stones. Remove by piercing the end of the date with a skewer and then squeezing the stone out or cut in half lengthways and remove the stone.

TO FREEZE
Pack in usable quantities in polythene bags. Seal, label and freeze.

STORAGE TIME: Up to 12 months.

TO DEFROST AND SERVE: Leave in their wrappings at room temperature for 2 hours to defrost.

USES: Use fresh whole or chopped in sweet and savoury salads. Alternatively, stuff them with cream cheese mixtures, or use in baking where required.

79

DUCKS

Ideally duckling should be 6 weeks to 3 months old and weigh 1-1.5 kg/2-3 lbs; and ducks should be up to 1 year old and weigh up to 3 kg/7 lbs for freezing.

SELECTING FOR FREEZING

Choose young plump birds. Older birds can be used for making pâtés and casseroles but it is not recommended that older birds are frozen for roasting.

PREPARATION FOR FREEZING

Pluck and hang if necessary. Singe small remaining feathers and hairs over a flame. Remove head and feet, and draw the entrails, separating the giblets (which should be frozen separately from the bird if a long storage life is desired).

TO FREEZE

Whole birds should be prepared as for cooking with legs and wings well trussed to the body to give a compact shape. Place a small pad of foil over any protruding bones so that they do not puncture the packaging. Wrap in a gusseted polythene bag taking care to mould around the duck, removing as much air as possible. Seal, label and freeze.

NB It is not advisable to stuff duck before freezing because the stuffing itself takes a long time to reach the desired low temperature, thus giving possible food spoilage organisms the time and warm conditions necessary for their growth. The storage time in the freezer would be reduced to that of the stuffing (little over a month) making unstuffed duck a much more desirable freezer product.

Pack giblets in a rigid container. Seal, label and freeze.

STORAGE TIME: 4-6 months for duck; 3 months for giblets.

TO DEFROST AND SERVE: ALL DUCKS MUST BE COMPLETELY DEFROSTED BEFORE COOKING. Defrost at room temperature for the times below (alternatively defrost in the refrigerator but the times will be 2-3 times longer):

Duckling about 6-8 hours
Small duck about 8-10 hours
Large duck about 14 hours

Giblets should be defrosted in their container in the refrigerator for about 12 hours.

USES: Duck can be roasted, plain or stuffed, and served with an apple sauce or other tart fruit sauce like cherry or orange – this counteracts the richness. If stuffing is not possible then consider serving the duck with a side salad of orange segments with crisp salad leaves. Older ducks can be casseroled or made into pâtés and terrines.

EELS

The eel is a firm fleshy fish that can weigh anything from 2-9 kg/5-20 lbs. The large ones often lack flavour and can be coarse and watery, whilst the smallest are too bony. Freshwater eels are not on the whole recommended for freezing. For sea water or Conger Eels the following procedure should be adopted:

SELECTING FOR FREEZING
Choose conger eels that weigh between 4-7 kg/10-15 lbs. Freeze within 24 hours of the catch.

PREPARATION FOR FREEZING: Skin, clean and remove the head. Cut into 7.5 cm/3 inch lengths, wash well and soak in lightly salted water. Pat dry with absorbent kitchen paper.

TO FREEZE: Interleave individual pieces (for easy removal) then pack in a polythene bag. Exclude as much air as possible. Seal, label and freeze.

STORAGE TIME: Up to 3 months.

TO DEFROST AND SERVE: Cook from frozen by gently poaching.

USES: Ideally used in soups and stews.

EGGS

Sometimes eggs are available on special offer and those that keep hens may find that they have a surplus from time to time.

SELECTING FOR FREEZING
Only freeze very fresh eggs. Do not freeze in their shells or as hard-boiled eggs since their shells are likely to crack due to expansion of the contents. Hard-boiled eggs do not freeze well as the white develops a granular and leathery texture which is generally considered unacceptable. The eggs should be taken out of their shells and stored according to requirements.

PREPARATION FOR FREEZING
Whole unbeaten eggs can be frozen individually in small foil or plastic

containers. Whole beaten eggs can be frozen in the same containers but with either the addition of 1.25 ml/¼ teaspoon salt or 2.5 ml/½ teaspoon sugar to maintain the texture. To freeze just yolks, mix 1.25 ml/¼ teaspoon of salt or sugar to 2 egg yolks to prevent the yolk from thickening.

TO FREEZE

Freeze the above egg mixtures in plastic boxes or ice cube containers. When the 'egg cubes' are frozen solid, remove from the trays and store in polythene bags, noting the cube volume on the packaging for easy measurement when using in recipes. Label 'salt' or 'sugar' for the appropriate savoury or sweet use. Egg whites may be packed and frozen in polythene boxes or ice cube trays, with or without the addition of salt or sugar, and can be whisked after defrosting at room temperature. If your eggs are supplied in egg boxes of the clear plastic type then a tip is to wash the box thoroughly then open freeze the egg white and yolk separately in the opened up boxes. When frozen the cubes can be popped out of the box and placed in polythene bags to save on freezer space.

STORAGE TIME: 6-9 months.

TO DEFROST AND SERVE: Eggs are best defrosted in the refrigerator for 3-4 hours but they can be defrosted at room temperature, which takes about 1½ hours.

USES: In baking, soufflés, mousses, cheesecakes, pastries, omelettes, scrambled eggs, baked eggs, stuffings, sauces, custards and meringues.

ELDERBERRIES

Elderberries are the fruit of the Elder and when ripe are superb for making jelly, wine and syrup. They are generally found wild in the hedgerows although there are some large-berried varieties that have been developed for garden cultivation.

SELECTING FOR FREEZING

Look out for elderberries that are dark in colour with a whitish bloom like grapes. A reddish tinge will indicate that they are still unripe. Pick the berries in bunches on a dry day.

PREPARATION FOR FREEZING

Separate the berries from their stalks by running a fork through the bunch. Pick out and discard any under-ripe berries. Do not wash unless very dirty or if you are going to make a sauce from them before freezing.

TO FREEZE

Freeze whole elderberries in either a free-flow or dry sugar pack. To make a free-flow pack, open freeze on trays until solid then transfer to polythene bags. Seal, label and return to the freezer. To make a dry sugar pack, pack in usable quantities in rigid containers, sprinkling each layer with sugar and allowing 100-175 g/4-6 oz sugar to 450 g/1 lb fruit. Seal, label and freeze. To make an elderberry sauce, cook in the minimum amount of water with sugar to taste until tender. Rub through a fine nylon sieve or purée in a blender or food processor then sieve. Pour in usable quantities into rigid containers leaving a 2 cm/¾ inch headspace. Seal, label and freeze.

STORAGE TIME: All types up to 12 months.

TO DEFROST AND SERVE: Leave whole elderberries to stand in their wrappings at room temperature for 2-3 hours. Elderberry sauce can be defrosted as whole elderberries or reheated from frozen over a very low heat, stirring frequently and adding a little extra water to prevent sticking.

USES: Use whole uncooked berries in fruit salads and summer puddings. Cook whole berries and use in pies and crumbles. Use elderberry sauce like cranberry sauce as an accompaniment to savoury dishes or for making ice creams, sorbets and mousses. The berries can also be used to make a juice for making jellies, wine and syrup.

FENNEL

Fennel is especially popular in Italian cooking. It is available as tightly packed heads consisting of the swollen leaf bases surrounding squat stems topped off with feathery green leaves. It has a delicate aniseed flavour and is delicious both raw and cooked.

SELECTING FOR FREEZING

Choose firm, tight heads with white leaf bases. The feathery green leaves should not be limp, nor the white base brown or discoloured.

PREPARATION FOR FREEZING

Trim away the feathery green fronds (they can be frozen separately as a herb). Scrub the outer leaves and scrape to remove any strings. Cut each head into quarters.

TO FREEZE

Blanch the quartered heads in boiling salted water for 3-5 minutes, according to size. Drain, cool in iced water, drain again and pat dry with absorbent kitchen paper. Pack in usable quantities in polythene bags. Seal, label and freeze.

STORAGE TIME: Up to 6 months.

TO DEFROST AND SERVE: Cook from frozen in boiling salted water for about 7 minutes until tender. Fennel can be used from frozen for soups, stews and casseroles. Use defrosted and thinly sliced raw in salads or stir-fried with other vegetables.

USES: As a vegetable accompaniment, serve plain or with a béchamel or cheese sauce or with a mixture of other cooked vegetables. Use in soups, stews and casseroles, in stir fries and raw in salads.

FIGS

Figs freeze very well and since they have a short season are well worth their freezer space. On sale in the late summer and early autumn there are green and purple-skinned varieties to choose from. The inner flesh can vary from white to purple and red.

SELECTING FOR FREEZING
Choose plump fruits which are soft and yield to a gentle squeeze. Skins can be slightly wrinkled but do take care that they are not bruised or split.

PREPARATION FOR FREEZING
Wipe carefully with a damp cloth then dry with absorbent kitchen paper. Freeze peeled or unpeeled as you like. If peeling, then peel with a sharp knife, taking care not to bruise. Ideally peel one fig at a time and immerse in the prepared sugar syrup.

TO FREEZE
Open freeze unpeeled figs until solid, then pack in rigid containers, seal, label and return to the freezer. Pack peeled figs into rigid containers and cover with a light sugar syrup (see page 25). Leave a 2 cm/¾ inch headspace, seal, label and freeze.

STORAGE TIME: Up to 12 months.

TO DEFROST AND SERVE: Leave unpeeled figs to stand in their wrappings at room temperature for 1½ hours then serve as fresh figs. Peeled figs can be defrosted as unpeeled figs or can be heated gently in a pan over a low heat to serve hot.

USES: Serve with cured meats as a starter, with cream as a dessert or in fruit salads.

FINNAN HADDIE

See *Smoked Haddock* (page 151)

FISH CAKES

Fish cakes, like fish croquettes, freeze very well.

PREPARATION FOR FREEZING
Prepare according to recipe, but be sure that the fish is absolutely fresh.

TO FREEZE
Open freeze on trays until solid, then place in polythene bags or rigid containers. Seal, label and return to the freezer.

STORAGE TIME: 1-2 months.

TO DEFROST AND SERVE: Either defrost slowly in the refrigerator for 6-8 hours or bake from frozen in a moderate oven (180°C/350°F/Gas 4) until cooked, depending upon the type of recipe.

USES: Serve as a main course dish with lemon wedges and perhaps a sauce. A tartare, tomato or cucumber sauce all go well.

FLANS

PASTRY FLANS
Shortcrust pastry flans, both sweet and savoury, can be made for freezing. However, flan cases are often better baked 'blind' depending upon the filling. Concerning filling, plain egg custard tends to separate out, though quiche type fillings are ideal.
  Flans with a puff pastry base are best cooked completely with filling. To prevent the pastry becoming soggy, when freezing both uncooked pastry and filling together, brush the inside of the flan with beaten egg white.

SPONGE FLANS
Sponge flans can be frozen either filled or not, dependent upon whether the filling is suitable for freezing. If the filling is glazed then freezing is not recommended and should be filled after defrosting.

TO FREEZE
Wrap very carefully since they are fragile. Pack in rigid boxes for extra protection. Seal, label and freeze.

❄ STORAGE TIME: Unfilled pastry and sponge cases 6 months; filled depends upon filling but usually 1-2 months.

TO DEFROST AND SERVE: Defrost unfilled baked pastry and sponge flan cases for 1 hour at room temperature. Refresh if wished in the oven. Unfilled and unbaked pastry cases can be cooked from frozen according to the recipe but add an extra 5 minutes cooking time. Filled flans should be defrosted in the refrigerator overnight, or for 2-5 hours, depending upon the nature of the filling.

FLOUNDER

This is a fish of the same family as brill, dab, sole and turbot. It is oval in shape and covered with tiny scales. Although a salt-water fish, it is often found in fresh water. It is ideally fried or steamed. For freezing follow the instructions for freezing COD (see page 69).

FRENCH BEANS

There are very many types of French beans available for the kitchen gardener and shopper alike from dwarf to kidney and stringless to round-podded (known better as bobbi beans). All freeze superbly and can also be frozen as part of a vegetable mixture or in a made-up dish (for example in a vegetable lasagne).

SELECTING FOR FREEZING

Home-grown beans can be harvested from June to September. Pick young and tender beans that are no longer than 10 cm/4 inches in length. A good indication of freshness is to try and snap one - if it snaps cleanly then undeniably it is very fresh. Imported and home-grown beans for the commercial market can often be too expensive for general home freezing but occasionally good bargains can be had at the beginning of the season around about June.

PREPARATION FOR FREEZING

Leave small beans whole, top and tail and wash under cold running water. Slice larger beans diagonally into 2.5 cm/1 inch lengths, removing any coarse side strings.

TO FREEZE

Grade whole beans according to size. Blanch whole and sliced beans separately. Blanch whole beans in boiling water for 3 minutes, drain, cool quickly in iced water, drain again and pat dry with absorbent kitchen paper. Open freeze on trays until solid, pack in usable quantities in

86

polythene bags, seal, label and return to the freezer. Blanch sliced beans for 2 minutes, drain, cool quickly in iced water, drain again and pat dry with absorbent kitchen paper. Open freeze on trays until solid, pack in usable quantities in polythene bags, seal, label and return to the freezer.

STORAGE TIME: Up to 12 months.

TO DEFROST AND SERVE: Cook beans from frozen in boiling salted water. Whole beans should be cooked for 7 minutes and sliced beans for 5 minutes. Drain to serve.

USES: Serve as a vegetable accompaniment tossed in melted butter and seasonings if you like. Use in salads, vegetable mixtures, casseroles, stir-fries and made-up dishes like curries.

GARLIC BREAD

Garlic or other flavoured breads, like herb, can be frozen.

PREPARATION FOR FREEZING
Make 2-3 cm/¾-1 inch cuts along a French or Vienna loaf to within 1-2 cm/½-¾ inch of the base. Spread creamed butter flavoured with garlic (herbs or cheese), generously between the slices.

TO FREEZE
Wrap tightly in heavy-duty foil. Seal, label and freeze.

STORAGE TIME: Up to 1 week, the crust begins to shell off after this time.

TO DEFROST AND SERVE: Cook from frozen. Place the garlic bread, wrapped in foil, in a moderately hot oven (200°C/400°F/Gas 6). A French stick takes about 20 minutes to defrost and cook through, a Vienna loaf about 30 minutes.

USES: Serve with soups and stews, pasta-type meals and at parties.

GATEAUX

See *Cakes* (page 53).

GIBLETS

Because the storage life of giblets is considerably less than for poultry or game itself, they should not be packed inside the carcass cavity of the bird or the storage time of the whole is reduced.

TO FREEZE
Either pack each bird's giblets separately in small polythene bags to use for gravy etc, or if a quantity of birds are being frozen at one time the livers may be frozen together in quantities enough to use in a recipe of their own, eg pâté.

STORAGE TIME: Up to 3 months.

TO DEFROST AND SERVE: Defrost giblets in their container in the refrigerator for about 12 hours.

USES: Use to make gravy and stocks or in a recipe to make pâtés, terrines, stuffings and forcemeats.

GLOBE ARTICHOKES

Globe artichokes freeze successfully. Look out for them in the shops from May onwards - they are best for freezing in July and August.

SELECTING FOR FREEZING
Only the best artichokes are worth freezing. The leaves should be stiff and only just slightly open. Avoid any that are fully open, discoloured or with fuzzy leaves.

PREPARATION FOR FREEZING
Remove the outer leaves and stalk then wash thoroughly. Also remove the hairy choke from the centre of the artichoke. Cut off the spiky tops of the leaves with a pair of scissors. Rub with a cut lemon to prevent discolouration.

TO FREEZE
Blanch whole artichokes in boiling water for 7-9 minutes, depending upon size; and hearts for 5 minutes. Add about 15 ml/1 tablespoon lemon juice to the blanching water to help retain a good colour. Drain, cool in iced water, drain again and pat dry with absorbent kitchen paper. Pack in rigid containers as the spiky leaves may pierce polythene bags. Seal, label and freeze.

STORAGE TIME: 12 months.

TO DEFROST AND SERVE: Cook from frozen in boiling water for about 5-10 minutes, according to size, until the base feels tender when pierced with a skewer and the leaves will pull away easily. Drain immediately and serve with the suggestions below.

USES: Serve globe artichokes as a starter with melted butter or Hollandaise sauce. Or serve hot or cold with a vinaigrette dressing. Alternatively, remove the inner leaves and fill with a savoury stuffing then bake in the oven. Artichoke hearts can be served as whole artichokes or can be added to salads, casseroles, omelettes, quiches and baked dishes.

GOOSE

Before the advent of the turkey, roast goose was the traditional dish to serve at Christmas and at harvest thanksgivings hence the name – Michaelmas Goose. Goose can be cooked in any way suitable for poultry in general, and when roasted is normally stuffed with sage and onion and served with an apple sauce.

The recommended size for home freezing is 3.5-4.5 kg/8-10 lbs. For freezing follow the instructions for freezing DUCKS (page 80).

GOOSEBERRIES

Perhaps the most popular type of gooseberry grown for eating is the Leveller. Sadly, this is not the best suitable for freezing so it is important to choose other varieties that are better such as Careless or Whinham's. The latter freeze superbly and also make delicious jams.

SELECTING FOR FREEZING

Look for fresh gooseberries in the spring and early summer. Choose slightly under-ripe specimens if you intend to freeze whole – soft juicy berries will disintegrate into a pulp in the freezer.

TO FREEZE

Gooseberries can be frozen as whole berries, as stewed berries and as gooseberry pulp.

Whole berries should be washed in iced water. Top and tail if you intend to put them in a dry sugar or syrup pack, if free-flow then don't bother. For a free-flow pack, open freeze on trays until solid, then pack, in usable quantities in polythene bags. Seal, label and return to the freezer.

For a dry sugar pack, pack the berries in usable quantities in rigid containers, sprinkling between each layer with sugar and allowing 100-175 g/4-6 oz sugar to every 450 g/1 lb fruit. Seal, label and freeze. For a syrup pack, pack the berries in usable quantities in rigid containers and cover with a medium sugar syrup (see page 25). Leave a 2 cm/¾ inch headspace. Seal, label and freeze.

To make stewed gooseberries, top and tail, then poach gently in a little water with sugar to taste. A few elderflower heads, tied in a muslin bag, give a wonderful flavour and aroma. Remove and discard the bag and cool quickly. Pack, in usable quantities, in rigid containers, leaving a 2 cm/¾ inch headspace. Seal, label and freeze.

To make a gooseberry pulp or purée, cook as for stewed gooseberries then purée in a blender or food processor. Cool and pack into rigid containers, in usable quantities, leaving a 2 cm/¾ inch headspace. Seal, label and freeze.

STORAGE TIME: 12 months.

TO DEFROST AND SERVE: Whole berries should be rubbed while frozen to remove the tops and tails and then can be used from frozen in pies, crumbles and other hot puddings. If required for jam making then allow to defrost at room temperature, in a single layer, for 1 hour.

Whole berries in sugar and syrup can also be treated the same way although a longer defrosting time may be required, more like 2-3 hours.

Stewed gooseberries can be reheated from frozen by cooking gently over a low heat and stirring frequently. Add a little extra water if required.

Gooseberry pulp should be defrosted in the refrigerator overnight or at room temperature for about 3 hours.

USES: Use whole berries to make jams and preserves, hot puddings, pies and crumbles; stewed gooseberries make a good pie or tart filling; gooseberry pulp can be used to make fools, sorbets, ice creams, mousses, sauces both sweet and savoury and a cheesecake topping.

GRAPEFRUIT

Grapefruit can be frozen in slices or segments for use at breakfast time, or to use as a starter, or in desserts.

For freezing follow the instructions for freezing ORANGES (page 117).

GRAPES

Good-quality grapes are available all year round so it should not be necessary to freeze on the basis of unavailability. However, a surplus or good bargain should not be missed and grapes do freeze well in a sugar syrup.

SELECTING FOR FREEZING
Choose firm but fully ripe fruit.

PREPARATION FOR FREEZING
Remove grapes from the bunch. Wash and dry. Large grapes should be skinned and deseeded.

TO FREEZE

Pack in rigid containers, in usable quantities. Cover with a medium sugar syrup (see page 25). Leave a 2 cm/¾ inch headspace. Seal, label and freeze.

STORAGE TIME: 12 months.

TO DEFROST AND SERVE: Defrost in the container allowing 6-7 hours in the refrigerator or 2-3 hours at room temperature.

USES: In fruit salads, flans, creams and as an accompaniment to some fish and chicken dishes.

GREENGAGES

Greengages are a yellowish-green variety of plum. The flesh is firm and the flavour is generally considered superior to other varieties of plums. Use for ices, mousses and fools - the tart greengage flavour also goes well in sauces and stuffings for serving with duck, goose and pork.

For freezing follow the instructions for freezing PLUMS (page 131).

GREY MULLET

Grey mullet is caught in shoals off the Cornish coast in early summer. The fish is silvery grey in colour, not unlike bass and is covered with large, broad scales. The flesh is white and firm and easy to digest. It can be cooked like haddock and cod.

For freezing follow the instructions for freezing BASS (see page 38).

GROUSE

Grouse is considered to be the most delicious of the game birds. It is in season from August to December but at its best from August to October. Young grouse can be roasted and grilled, older birds should be casseroled or braised.

For freezing follow the instructions for freezing PHEASANTS (see page 128).

GUAVAS

The guava is a tropical fruit which varies in size from being as small as a cherry to as large as an apple. It is said to taste like a cross between a melon and a strawberry but the flavour varies considerably from one variety to another. Its flesh also varies considerably from white through to yellow, then pink and even crimson.

SELECTING FOR FREEZING

Buy only firm, young fruit with shiny unblemished skins.

PREPARATION FOR FREEZING

Peel and cut in half lengthways and scoop out the seeds with a spoon. Leave as halves or cut the flesh into dice or slices.

TO FREEZE

Guavas can be frozen as halves or slices in either a dry sugar pack, a syrup pack or as a purée. To prepare a dry sugar pack, put the halves or slices in usable quantities in rigid containers, sprinkling between each layer with sugar to taste. Seal, label and freeze. To make a syrup pack, place halves or slices in usable quantities in rigid containers and cover with a light sugar syrup (see page 25). Leave a 2 cm/¾ inch headspace. Seal, label and freeze. To make a guava purée, cook the halves or slices in a light sugar syrup made with 100 g/4 oz sugar and 600 ml/1 pint water for about 30 minutes until tender. Mash the fruit with a wooden spoon and allow to cool. Purée in a blender or food processor then sieve. Pour into a rigid container, leaving a 2 cm/¾ inch headspace. Seal, label and freeze.

STORAGE TIME: Up to 6 months.

TO DEFROST AND SERVE: Defrost dry sugar pack halves and slices at room temperature for 3-4 hours. Alternatively, mix with other fruit to make pies, flans or crumbles and allow a little extra cooking time for defrosting. Cook sugar syrup pack guavas from frozen until tender over a low heat.

USES: Serve hot or chilled guavas in syrup as a dessert with pouring cream or yogurt. Alternatively use chilled in fresh fruit salads. Guavas can also be used in pie, flan and pudding mixtures for baking.

GUINEA FOWL

The guinea fowl is a domestic fowl, about the size of a pheasant and similar in flavour. It is prepared and cooked in any way suitable for chicken.

For freezing follow the instructions for freezing CHICKENS but only store for up to 6 months (page 63).

HADDOCK

Haddock is a round sea fish of the cod family. It has a greyish skin and is easily distinguished by a black line which runs down each side of it and it has a black fingermark behind each gill. Legend calls this Saint Peter's mark. Haddock can usually be bought all year round but is at its best from November to February. It is sold whole, in cutlets, steaks or fillets. The flesh is firm and white and the fish lends itself to various ways of cooking. It is very good stuffed and baked. Prepare and cook like cod.

For freezing follow the instructions for freezing COD (see page 69)

HAKE

Hake is a large, round fish caught off the western coasts of England and in the Irish Channel. In appearance it is similar to cod, but has a sharp pointed face like a pike. The fish crumbles easily and the bones are easy to remove, so it is particularly suitable for dishes like fish mousse, soufflé and creams. It can also be cooked like cod or turbot.

For freezing follow the instructions for freezing COD (see page 69).

HALIBUT

This is a flat fish similar in appearance to turbot and available mainly from August through to April. It grows to a great size and is generally sold in steaks, cutlets or fillets. Chicken halibut is a smaller variety only weighing up to 1.5 kg/3 lbs and is considered better in flavour. Prepare and use like cod and turbot.

For freezing follow the instructions for freezing COD (see page 69).

HAMBURGERS

See *Burgers* (page 50)

HARE

Hare is a wild animal classed as game and in season from the end of August till the beginning of March. To develop the game flavour the hare should be well hung and the inside not removed for 4-5 days. A young hare, called a leveret, is suitable for roasting, but an old hare should be jugged, ie cooked slowly in stock or red wine or used for making soup.

For freezing follow the instructions for freezing RABBITS (see page 138).

HERB BREAD

Herb bread freezes superbly and can be served with soups, pasta-type meals and at parties.

For freezing follow the instructions for freezing GARLIC BREAD (page 87).

HERBS

Whether growing your own or buying fresh herbs, it is always handy to freeze down any excess to immediate requirements for later use, especially for when your favourite herb is out of season.

Home-grown herbs should be picked in their prime, when the leaves are young and tender and before the plant begins to flower. Cut them early in the morning for best results. Freeze in one of the following ways:

METHOD 1

Wash if necessary, shake off excess moisture, pat dry, then chop leaves, including some stalks for added flavour. Pack into polythene bags or rigid containers, seal, label and freeze. Spoonfuls can be removed as required and the pack returned to the freezer.

METHOD 2

Wash if necessary, shake off excess moisture, chop herbs and place in ice cube trays until almost full. Top up with a little cold water and freeze until solid. Alternatively the herbs can be liquidised. Transfer into polythene bags or rigid containers, seal, label and return to the freezer. Frozen cubes can be added to hot dishes, or left to defrost in a fine strainer if preferred.

METHOD 3

Whole sprigs can be washed if necessary, dried and put straight into tiny polythene bags, sealed, labelled and frozen. If whole sprigs require to be chopped after freezing, this is easily done by just rubbing frozen sprigs (as soon as they are taken from the freezer) between the palms of your hands. The leaves will crumble ready for use. Blanching is not necessary but one or two herbs such as balm and chervil benefit from being blanched for 1 minute.

STORAGE TIME: Up to 6 months.

HERRINGS

Herrings are one of the most nourishing and probably the most inexpensive fish caught off English shores. Available all the year round, but best in early summer. It can be baked, fried or grilled. For freezing follow the instructions for freezing TROUT (see page 163).

HORSERADISH

Horseradish is a hot, pungent root which can grow wild or be cultivated. It is used grated as a condiment and is especially good with roast beef and some smoked fish like smoked trout. For freezing it can be frozen with or without cream (the cream being added later in the latter case after defrosting).

SELECTING FOR FREEZING

Use only roots that are this years current growth – old ones will tend to be woody.

PREPARATION FOR FREEZING

Peel, wash, pat dry and grate the root. Either mix together 30 ml/2 tablespoons grated horseradish with 10 ml/2 teaspoons lemon juice, 10 ml/2 teaspoons sugar and 75 ml/5 tablespoons double cream. Or mix grated horseradish with sugar and wine vinegar to taste. (Add cream after defrosting). Pack, in small usable quantities, in rigid containers. Leave a 2 cm/¾ inch headspace. Seal, label and freeze.

STORAGE TIME: 2 months with cream; 6 months without cream.

TO DEFROST AND SERVE: Defrost overnight in the refrigerator.

USES: Use with roast beef, smoked fish like trout and mackerel, shellfish and in salads.

HUSS

See *Rock Salmon* (page 143)

ICE CREAMS

A freezer gives the enthusiastic cook a greater opportunity to try her hand at making her own ice cream, particularly unusual ones or ones using fresh fruit from the kitchen garden or market. Experiment with any good recipe - the best ones use cream, egg yolks and sometimes gelatine and flavourings as you like. Needless to say home freezer ownership has probably helped to increase the enormous variety of ice creams available for purchase. Buying large quantities also offers considerable savings in money. As the container is used it is advisable to cover the cut surface with foil to avoid ice crystals from forming with consequent loss of flavour and texture.

TO FREEZE

Follow a reliable recipe using the best and freshest ingredients available. Pour into rigid containers and freeze until firm (following any specific instructions about beating half-way through the freezing process if necessary). Seal and label. Freeze any commercially prepared ice cream as soon as possible after purchase so that it does not have the opportunity to defrost. Never on any account re-freeze ice cream if it has defrosted. It is a highly perishable substance and especially heat sensitive. Shrinkage and loss of texture will be quickly apparent, followed by being potentially unsafe to eat.

STORAGE TIME: Up to 3 months or according to instructions on the pack.

TO DEFROST AND SERVE: Soft-scoop varieties can be scooped and served straight from the freezer. Home-made and non-soft-scoop varieties should be placed in the refrigerator for 10-20 minutes before serving to soften slightly and to enhance flavour and texture.

USES: For serving with puddings and desserts, as an integral ingredient for recipes like a filling for cakes and gâteaux and Baked Alaska.

ICINGS

Icings and fillings which freeze well are butter cream, whipped cream (see page 74), glacé icing and royal icing.

PREPARATION AND SELECTION FOR FREEZING

Butter cream freezes well and can be flavoured as desired (with chocolate or coffee for example). It can be put in or on a cake before freezing without risk providing the wrap is sufficiently firm to prevent damage. Glacé icing or water icing freezes satisfactorily but used on the surface of a cake is inclined to crack when defrosted. If in doubt and presentation is all important then ice after defrosting the cake.

Royal icing must be very carefully wrapped to protect it and to exclude moisture. Given these conditions it freezes well but it is usually adequate to keep it in an airtight tin.

TO FREEZE

Pack butter cream in small rigid containers so that the desired amount can be spooned out at one time. Alternatively, pipe and open freeze until solid, then store in a rigid box and lift out to use for cake decorations. Place on the cake and then allow to defrost.

STORAGE TIME: Up to 3 months.

TO DEFROST AND SERVE: Defrost all icings at room temperature. A 225 g/8 oz quantity of buttercream will take about 2-3 hours to defrost completely.

USES: For cake fillings, toppings and decorations.

JAM

An excellent uncooked jam can be made and stored in the freezer. It is basically crushed fresh fruit with sugar, lemon juice and liquid pectin. It is not as 'set' as conventional jam and once defrosted has a life of about 2 weeks if kept in the refrigerator.

PREPARATION FOR FREEZING

The basic recipe needs 450 g/1 lb fruit (apricots, blackberries, cherries, peaches, plums, raspberries or strawberries for example), 900 g/2 lb caster sugar, 5 ml/1 teaspoon lemon juice and 100 ml/4 fl oz liquid pectin. Skin any thick-skinned fruits, stone and mash with sugar and lemon juice. Leave to stand for 20 minutes, stirring occasionally. Stir in the pectin and mix thoroughly.

TO FREEZE

Spoon in usable quantities into rigid containers, leaving a 2 cm/¾ inch headspace. Seal and label. Leave at room temperature for several hours before putting into the refrigerator for 24-48 hours to set, then freeze.

STORAGE TIME: Up to 12 months.

TO DEFROST AND SERVE: Defrost overnight in the refrigerator and stir well before serving.

USES: As for conventional jam.

JELLIES

Jellies which are so quickly prepared are not really recommended for the freezer. As they are sweet they do retain their setting quality but do tend to lose their clarity and have a granular cloudy appearance when defrosted. This is especially apparent when a thin layer is used as a glaze or at the bottom of a mould.

JERUSALEM ARTICHOKES

These knobbly, tuberous vegetables are not really artichokes at all although some say their flavour resembles that of the artichoke.

SELECTING FOR FREEZING

Choose firm tubers with as few knobbles as possible for easy preparation. Avoid any that look damaged in any way since they are prone to attack from worms and slugs. They are in season from late October right through to Spring.

PREPARATION FOR FREEZING

Prepare in small batches since the tubers do have a tendency to discolour. Scrub thoroughly, removing the smallest knobbles. Jerusalem artichokes can be frozen as cubes and slices or as a purée. To prepare cubes and slices, peel thinly and cut into cubes or slice thickly, then place in iced water with a little lemon juice or vinegar added to prevent discolouration. To make a purée, cook the artichokes in boiling water for about 15 minutes until tender. Drain and leave until cool enough to handle. Pull or rub off the skins and purée in a blender or food processor until smooth.

TO FREEZE

Blanch cubes and slices in boiling water for 2 minutes. Drain and cool rapidly in iced water then pat dry with absorbent kitchen paper. Pack in usable quantities in polythene bags. Seal, label and freeze. Pack artichoke purée in usable quantities in rigid containers, leaving a 2 cm/¾ inch headspace. Seal, label and freeze.

STORAGE TIME: Up to 3 months.

TO DEFROST AND SERVE: Cook cubes and slices from frozen in boiling salted water for about 3 minutes until just tender. Use hot or leave to cool and serve cold. Frozen cubes and slices can be added to casseroles and stews about 10 minutes before the end of cooking. Leave artichoke purée to stand in its container at room temperature for about 2 hours; use as you like.

USES: Jerusalem artichoke slices and pieces are delicious as a vegetable accompaniment if covered with a cheese, tomato or parsley sauce. Alternatively, toss cold pieces or slices in a dressing and add to salad mixtures. An oil and vinegar or mustard-based dressing and a mayonnaise or tartare-style sauce all work well. Use Jerusalem artichoke purée to make soups.

KALE

Kale is a hardy green vegetable with crinkled leaves, of the cabbage family. It is cooked and served like cabbage.

SELECTING FOR FREEZING
Choose only young, tender tightly-curled leaves; do not use dry, discoloured or coarse ones. Look out for bargains from December onwards.

PREPARATION FOR FREEZING
Remove the leaves from the stalks and wash the leaves thoroughly.

TO FREEZE
Blanch in boiling water for 1-2 minutes. Drain, cool in iced water, drain again and pat dry with absorbent kitchen paper. Chop after blanching if you like. Pack, in usable quantities, into polythene bags. Seal, label and freeze.

STORAGE TIME: 9 months.

TO DEFROST AND SERVE: Cook from frozen in boiling salted water for 8 minutes. Drain and serve with melted butter if desired.

USES: As a vegetable accompaniment with or without a cheese sauce; as a substitute for spinach and as an ingredient in a vegetable stir-fry.

KIDNEYS

It is important that kidneys and all offal are prepared and frozen quickly.

PREPARATION FOR FREEZING
Prepare as for cooking, coring kidneys and removing their jacket of fat (if not removed this will reduce the storage time considerably because the fat can turn rancid). Wash and dry with a clean cloth.

TO FREEZE
Wrap in heavy-duty foil; each kidney can be interleaved for easy removal first if you like. Seal, label and freeze. Ox kidney however, is best diced and frozen in rigid containers. Seal, label and freeze.

STORAGE TIME: Up to 3 months.

TO DEFROST AND SERVE: Defrost in the refrigerator, in the wrappings overnight or for 8-12 hours, depending upon quantity.

USES: Kidneys can be grilled, sautéed or braised and used in breakfast grills, stuffings, pâtés and terrines.

KIPPERS

Kippers are smoked herrings and should be plump, juicy and pale if properly smoked. Avoid those with a bright dye to disguise inadequate treatment. Kippers are sold whole, usually in pairs, or as fillets. They can be used to make pâté and naturally can be eaten grilled for breakfast.

For freezing follow the instructions for freezing SMOKED HADDOCK (see page 151).

KIWIFRUIT

Kiwifruit can be frozen but because they have a high water content they do tend to collapse on defrosting. If you are able to buy cheaply and have too many to eat fresh, then prepare and freeze in the following way:

PREPARATION FOR FREEZING
Peel off the furry brown skin, then halve or slice.

TO FREEZE
Open freeze until solid on trays, then pack into rigid containers for fresh use. Seal, label and return to the freezer.
  Alternatively place in usable quantities in rigid containers and cover with a light sugar syrup (see page 25) with the addition of 45 ml/3 tablespoons lemon juice to each 600 ml/1 pint syrup. Leave a 2 cm/¾ inch headspace. Seal, label and freeze.

STORAGE TIME: 12 months.

TO DEFROST AND SERVE: Serve slightly defrosted if used on ice cream or as a starter or sweet when packed dry. Defrost in the unopened container if prepared in syrup for about 3 hours at room temperature.

USES: In fruit salads, as a starter or dessert with a vinaigrette dressing or whipped cream, for topping cakes, gâteaux and cheesecakes and for serving with some meats, eg lamb chops.

KOHLRABI

Kohlrabi is a root vegetable used in the same way as turnips. There are three varieties, white, green and purple. All freeze well. Look out for them in the shops in the autumn.

SELECTING FOR FREEZING
Choose small, young and tender kohlrabi with well-shaped firm stems.

PREPARATION FOR FREEZING
Trim off the stalks and the leaves; wash and peel thinly then cut into 2.5 cm/1 inch slices.

TO FREEZE
Blanch in boiling water for 2 minutes. Drain, cool in iced water, drain again and pat dry with absorbent kitchen paper. Pack in usable quantities in polythene bags or rigid containers. Seal, label and freeze.

STORAGE TIME: 12 months.

TO DEFROST AND SERVE: Cook from frozen in boiling water for 5-6 minutes or until tender.

USES: Serve as a vegetable accompaniment in a cream or mild cheese sauce or toss in butter and parsley. Use without further cooking in salads; or coated in batter and deep fried.

KUMQUAT

This is the tiniest of all the citrus fruits, being about the size of a large olive. It has a bitter-sweet flavour which makes it most versatile. It can be eaten whole, including the bright, thin, orange-coloured skin.

PREPARATION FOR FREEZING
Wash and leave whole or slice thickly with the skin on.

TO FREEZE
Open freeze whole fruit on trays until solid, then pack, in usable quantities, in polythene bags. Seal, label and return to the freezer.
 Pack sliced in rigid containers, sprinkling sugar between each layer to taste. Seal, label and freeze.
 Alternatively, cover with a medium sugar syrup (see page 25). Leave a 2 cm/¾ inch headspace. Seal, label and freeze.

STORAGE TIME: Up to 12 months.

❄ TO DEFROST AND SERVE: Leave to stand in the container at room temperature for 2 hours.

USES: Use whole and dry sugar pack kumquats in preserves and fruit salads. Serve sugar syrup packs as a dessert with cream or ice cream. Kumquat is also excellent served with duck as a substitute for orange.

LAMB

A whole lamb is an ideal buy for the home freezer owner as it gives a good variety of roasting, grilling and slow cooking meat in one purchase and is not a large quantity of meat, the average size of a whole lamb being 13-18 kg/30-40 lbs in weight.

SELECTING FOR FREEZING

The cuts obtained are leg, loin and chump, best end of neck, breast, middle neck, scrag, shoulder and kidney. Discuss with your supplier how you would like the meat butchering, ie would you like the loin left whole for a roast or cut into loin chops? Is the shoulder too big if left whole? Do you want the breast boned for stuffing etc? Lamb should be hung for 5-7 days before freezing. Remember that lamb bought in the spring and early summer is also likely to be more expensive that that bought in the late summer or autumn. For information a whole lamb will take up about 42 litres/1½ cu ft of space in your freezer.

New Zealand lamb is usually slightly cheaper than British. It is shipped in an already frozen state and so it is important to be sure when you purchase it that it has not been allowed to defrost. The butcher can still joint it to your requirements and will probably package it for you ready to be put straight into your freezer.

Joints will include the shoulder (whole and halved); breast; leg (whole and halved); loin (whole and halved into best loin and chump end); saddle (both loins joined together by backbone); best end of neck, crown roast and Guard of Honour (two best ends tied together).

Chops, cutlets and steaks will come from the following: the breast will be cut into riblets; the fillet end cut into 2.5 cm/1 inch steaks; the loin will be divided into loin and chump chops; the best end of neck will be divided into cutlets; and large cutlets from the same will be boned to make noisettes.

Boneless cubes and pieces of lamb will come from the shoulder and the leg. Cubes and pieces with bone will come from the middle neck and scrag.

Minced lamb usually comes from boneless meat from the shoulder.

PREPARATION FOR FREEZING AND TO FREEZE

JOINTS (for roasting/slow roasting): To help with carving and to economise on freezer space, shoulder, breast and leg joints may be boned, rolled and tied (but do not stuff before freezing). Ask the butcher to chine the loin, which can also be boned if you wish. Saw off any protruding bone ends and remove surplus fat. Pad bones with foil.

Wrap individual joints in cling film or foil, then overwrap in polythene bags. Exclude as much air as possible. Seal, label and freeze.

CHOPS, CUTLETS AND STEAKS (for grilling/frying and barbecuing): Trim off bone ends, any surplus fat and skin. Pad bones with foil. Wrap individually in cling film or foil with interleave, then pack together in polythene bags. Exclude as much air as possible. Seal, label and freeze.

CUBES AND PIECES (for casseroling/pies/sautéeing/stewing): Trim off surplus fat, sinews and gristle. Cut boneless meat into 2.5 cm/1 inch cubes if not already done. Pack cubes in usable quantities in polythene bags. Exclude as much air as possible. Seal, label and freeze. Pack any bony pieces in rigid containers, seal, label and freeze.

MINCED LAMB: Leave loose or shape into burgers, meatballs or patties etc. Pack loose mince in usable quantities in polythene bags. Exclude as much air as possible. Seal, label and freeze. To freeze burgers, patties and meatballs see BURGERS (page 50).

STORAGE TIME: Joints for up to 12 months; chops, cutlets and steaks for up to 12 months; cubes and pieces for up to 8 months; and minced lamb for 3 months.

TO DEFROST AND SERVE

JOINTS: Thaw in their wrappings at room temperature for 6-8 hours per kg/3-4 hours per lb, then cook as fresh. Small joints under 1.5 kg/3 lbs and on the bone can be cooked from frozen for approximately twice the usual time until 85°C/185°F is registered on a meat thermometer. Do not cook boned and rolled joints from frozen.

CHOPS, CUTLETS AND STEAKS: Thaw in their wrappings at room temperature for 2-3 hours, or in the refrigerator overnight, then cook as for fresh. Alternatively grill or fry from frozen, allowing extra time and brushing liberally with oil.

CUBES AND PIECES: Thaw in their wrappings at room temperature until the pieces separate, then cook as for fresh allowing a little extra time and using the thawed juices.

MINCED LAMB: Partially defrost loose mince in its wrappings in the refrigerator, then cook as for fresh, stirring well to prevent sticking. Cook burgers, meatballs and patties from frozen.

USES: Lamb is a most versatile meat and can be roasted, slow roasted, grilled, fried, casseroled, sautéed, stewed, barbecued, stir-fried and used to make countless dishes where it is baked.

LARD

Lard may be frozen in the same way as butter but is really only worth the freezer space if bought cheaply or if rendered when pork is being home butchered and prepared for the freezer.

For freezing follow the instructions for freezing BUTTER (page 51).

LEEKS

The leek is a winter vegetable with an onion flavour, best from November to March.

SELECTING FOR FREEZING

Choose thin, young leeks with a good fresh colour.

PREPARATION FOR FREEZING

Cut off excess green leaves and the root; it is easier to be sure of removal of grit if sliced.

TO FREEZE

Blanch in boiling water, 2 minutes for slices, 3 minutes for whole leeks. Drain, cool quickly in iced water, drain again and pat dry with absorbent kitchen paper. Pack, in usable quantities, in polythene bags or rigid containers. Seal, label and freeze.

STORAGE TIME: 6 months.

TO DEFROST AND SERVE: Cook from frozen for 5-10 minutes, depending upon size.

USES: Use as a vegetable accompaniment with a cheese sauce if liked, in soups, stews, casseroles and stir-fries.

LEMONS

Lemons can often be bought very cheaply in bulk and since they have so many uses are worth freezing when prices are low. Their fresh citrus taste can be used in countless sweet and savoury dishes and both the rind and the flesh are valuable for the enthusiastic cook.

For freezing follow the instructions for freezing ORANGES (see page 117).

LETTUCE

Lettuce cannot be frozen as a salad vegetable because of its high water content but it can be frozen as a purée for use in soups or as hearts and leaves for serving as a vegetable accompaniment.

SELECTING FOR FREEZING
Select firm, well-developed heads of lettuce for freezing.

PREPARATION FOR FREEZING
Remove any coarse outer leaves and the root. Wash well and separate the leaves until a small heart remains.

TO FREEZE
Blanch for 2 minutes or cook until tender and liquidise. Drain and pat dry the leaves and heart with absorbent kitchen paper. Pack, in usable quantities, in polythene bags. Seal, label and freeze. Spoon purée into rigid containers, allowing a 2 cm/¾ inch headspace. Seal, label and freeze.

STORAGE TIME: 6 months.

TO DEFROST AND SERVE: Cook from frozen, place the leaves and heart in a buttered ovenproof dish with a lid and cook until hot and tender. Alternatively, heat the purée with milk and/or cream and seasonings to make a soup.

USES: As a vegetable accompaniment. Serve with a Hollandaise, Espagnole or cheese sauce. As a hot or chilled soup.

LIMES

Limes, like oranges and lemons, have countless uses in the cook's repertoire. However, they can often bring a touch of sophistication to a recipe over and above that of the lemon or orange. They are also essential in Thai and oriental cooking which has enjoyed great popularity in recent times. Consider freezing some away when bargains appear in the market place.

For freezing follow the instructions for freezing ORANGES (see page 117).

LIVER

Liver, like all offal, should be prepared and frozen quickly.

PREPARATION FOR FREEZING

Prepare as for cooking. Liver is best sliced before packaging. Wash well then dry with a clean cloth.

TO FREEZE

Interleave slices of liver, then overwrap with heavy-duty foil. Pack in usable quantities. Seal, label and freeze.

STORAGE TIME: Up to 3 months.

TO DEFROST AND SERVE: Defrost in the wrappings in the refrigerator for about 8 hours. Use as for fresh.

USES: Fry with onions and bacon, use to make pâtés, terrines and other made-up dishes, cook and then chop to add interest to stuffings.

LOBSTER

There are several varieties of lobster which vary in size quite dramatically and are priced and prized accordingly.

SELECTING FOR FREEZING

Buy fresh live or cooked lobsters that have not previously been frozen. Specimens should be heavy for their size and have a good firm flesh, shiny shell and clean smell. Lobsters are available all year round but at their best from April to August.

PREPARATION FOR FREEZING

Lobster must be absolutely fresh and freshly boiled and cooled before freezing. Boil and cool in the usual way.

TO FREEZE

For best results closely wrap whole cooked lobster in heavy-gauge polythene or foil. Seal, label and freeze. Alternatively, split the shell in half lengthwise, remove the tail and claw meat, cut into neat pieces and pack in a polythene bag or rigid container. Seal, label and freeze.

STORAGE TIME: Up to 1 month.

TO DEFROST AND SERVE: Defrost in the wrappings for 6-8 hours in the refrigerator.

USES: Lobster can be boiled, baked and grilled in recipes. It can also be served cold with a mayonnaise or cucumber sauce.

LOGANBERRIES

The loganberry is a fruit very similar to the raspberry in appearance, but probably a cross between a blackberry and a raspberry. It has a large core which comes away easily when the fruit is gathered. Loganberries can be eaten raw or in desserts wherever raspberries are used and makes excellent jam and purées for fools and ice creams.

For freezing follow the instructions for freezing RASPBERRIES (page 139).

LYCHEES

The lychee is a tropical fruit which originated from China. It is normally only available fresh between December and February, so it is often worth having a few in the freezer for special occasions.

SELECTING FOR FREEZING
Look for nuts with a reddish-brown hue – if the casing is a dull brown they are well past their best.

PREPARATION FOR FREEZING
Remove the outer casing and squeeze out the central stone (if you like but this is not necessary).

TO FREEZE
Place in rigid containers, in usable quantities, and cover with a medium sugar syrup (see page 25) adding 15 ml/1 tablespoon lemon juice to every 600 ml/1 pint syrup. Leave a 2 cm/¾ inch headspace. Seal, label and freeze.

STORAGE TIME: 12 months.

TO DEFROST AND SERVE: Defrost slowly in the refrigerator and serve while still frosted in a fruit salad or with ice cream.

MACKEREL

The mackerel is a long, slender salt-water fish with an iridescent skin. It is a fatty, dark-fleshed fish that is available all year round but best from October to March. It lends itself particularly well to barbecuing, baking and grilling, although it can be marinated and eaten raw with plenty of lemon juice to counteract its richness.

For freezing follow the instructions for freezing TROUT (see page 163) but freeze within 12 hours of the catch.

MANDARINS

Mandarins, like tangerines and clementines, are small citrus fruits that have only a short season so they are well worth freezing so that their flavours can be enjoyed at other times of the year. The very loose skin which is easily peeled also makes this an easy task.

SELECTING FOR FREEZING
Buy shiny, firm fruit with plump, never dry or shrivelled-looking skins. Choose specimens that weigh heavy for their size – it is a sure sign that they are juicy not dry or pithy.

PREPARATION FOR FREEZING
Peel, then separate into segments, removing any excess pith and any visible pips if necessary.

TO FREEZE
Pack in usable quantities in rigid containers, sprinkling between each layer with sugar to taste. Alternatively, cover the segments with a medium sugar syrup (see page 25). Seal, label and freeze.

STORAGE TIME: Freeze for up to 12 months.

TO DEFROST AND SERVE: Defrost frozen mandarin segments in their container for about 2 hours at room temperature.

USES: Use in fruit salads, breakfast citrus dishes or fruit-based desserts.

MANGETOUT

This is a variety of pea that is picked before the pea itself is fully formed and is eaten like a French bean, whole with the pod. It is a traditional Chinese vegetable, popular in the East for centuries and has now become a regular favourite in the West. It has a crisp texture and the subtle flavour of peas.

SELECTING FOR FREEZING

Select when the pod is tender and flat and the peas have not started to form. If they have begun to swell then the pod will be stringy.

PREPARATION FOR FREEZING

Top and tail, and string if necessary.

TO FREEZE

Blanch in boiling water for 1 minute. Drain, cool in iced water, drain again and pat dry with absorbent kitchen paper. Open freeze on trays until solid, then pack into polythene bags, seal, label and return to the freezer.

STORAGE TIME: 12 months.

TO DEFROST AND SERVE: Cook from frozen in boiling water for 3-5 minutes. Toss in melted butter and seasonings to serve. Also can be stir-fried with other vegetables.

MANGOES

The mango is a fruit of Indian origin about the size of a large pear. In the early stages it is dark green in colour, but turns a deep orange as it ripens and then has a pleasantly sweet flavour, not unlike a peach or apricot. It is available from January to September.

SELECTING FOR FREEZING

Choose ripe mangoes that are neither squashy nor too firm.

PREPARATION FOR FREEZING

Wash, peel and slice or dice into cubes.

TO FREEZE

Place in usable quantities in rigid containers and cover with a light sugar syrup (see page 25) to which 15 ml/1 tablespoon lemon juice has been added for every 600 ml/1 pint syrup. Leave a 2 cm/¾ inch headspace. Seal, label and freeze.

STORAGE TIME: 12 months.

TO DEFROST AND SERVE: Defrost slowly overnight in the refrigerator.

USES: Use as part of a fruit salad, or purée to make a sauce to pour over ice cream. Alternatively, strain from the syrup and use to make a chutney.

MARGARINE

Margarine is only really worth freezing if purchased cheaply and plenty of freezer storage space is available.

For freezing follow the instructions for freezing BUTTER (page 51).

MARROW

Because of their high water content, fully-grown marrows are not ideal for freezing, but are quite successful frozen as a stuffed vegetable dish. Young marrows, slightly bigger than courgettes, can be frozen and cooked in the same way as courgettes. Serve as an accompanying vegetable with chopped tomatoes or a cheese sauce if you like.

For freezing follow the instructions for freezing COURGETTES (page 71).

MAYONNAISE

As mayonnaise is an emulsion it is unstable at low temperatures and tends to separate out, making it unpleasant to eat and therefore unacceptable for home freezing.

MEAT LOAVES

Meat loaves freeze well. Follow your regular recipe.

PREPARATION AND TO FREEZE
Cool rapidly then wrap in heavy-duty foil. Seal, label and freeze.

STORAGE TIME: Up to 1 month.

TO DEFROST AND SERVE: Defrost overnight or for at least 6-8 hours in the refrigerator. Reheat in a moderate oven 180°C/350°F/Gas 4, covered in foil, if you wish to serve warm. It will take 25-40 minutes, depending upon size.

MEAT PIES

Meat pies can be frozen successfully.

TO FREEZE

Prepare and cook as usual. Wrap carefully in heavy-duty foil and protect the tops with an inverted paper or aluminium foil plate. Seal, label and freeze.

STORAGE TIME: 3-4 months.

TO DEFROST AND SERVE: Leave to defrost at room temperature for 2-4 hours, depending upon size. If required hot, reheat in the oven at a moderate temperature, 180°C/350°F/Gas 4 for 30-40 minutes, or until very hot.

MELONS

Since melons have a relatively high sugar content they do freeze successfully, but are only best stored in a light sugar syrup pack.

SELECTING FOR FREEZING

Choose specimens at the optimum point of ripeness.

PREPARATION FOR FREEZING

Halve, deseed, cut into slices, cubes or balls of a uniform size.

TO FREEZE

Pack in usable quantities, in rigid containers and cover with a light sugar syrup (see page 25). Leave a 2 cm/¾ inch headspace. Seal, label and freeze.

STORAGE TIME: Up to 6 months.

TO DEFROST AND SERVE: Defrost slowly overnight in the refrigerator.

USES: With other citrus fruits at breakfast time or to make a Florida cocktail; with shellfish in starters; with fresh fruit in salads; and puréed to make a sorbet or water ice.

MERINGUES

Meringues freeze well, any dehydration aiding their crispness. Their high sugar content means they can be virtually eaten directly from the freezer, though it's true that they do store equally as well in an airtight tin.

TO FREEZE

Take care with packaging since meringues are fragile, especially take care with meringue shell cases. Pack in a rigid container for safety. Seal, label and freeze.

STORAGE TIME: Up to 12 months.

TO DEFROST AND SERVE: Remove from the freezer and allow to stand for 5-10 minutes before filling or serving.

MILK

As long-life milk is available, it is hardly necessary to freeze fresh milk.

SELECTING FOR FREEZING

Ordinary fresh milk does not freeze successfully as it contains less than 40% butterfat and tends to separate on defrosting. Homogenised milk will freeze fairly well because of the homogenising process, but even so, use only really fresh homogenised milk.

PREPARATION AND TO FREEZE

Do not freeze milk in glass bottles as they may crack or shatter as the liquid expands on freezing. Pack milk in plastic or waxed containers leaving about a 2.5 cm/1 inch headspace to allow for expansion. Homogenised milk bought in waxed cartons can be frozen as purchased.

STORAGE TIME: 4 weeks.

TO DEFROST AND SERVE: Slow defrosting in the refrigerator gives the best results, but if the milk is to be used for cooking it can be defrosted more quickly at room temperature or heated gently in a saucepan.

MOUSSES

Mousse is a very satisfactory food for freezing – both sweet and savoury freeze well.

TO FREEZE

Do not decorate before freezing. Wrap tightly in heavy-duty foil, seal, label and freeze.

STORAGE TIME: 2 months.

TO DEFROST AND SERVE: Defrost in the refrigerator overnight. Decorate after freezing.

MULBERRIES

Mulberries are the fruit of the mulberry tree, resembling a large blackberry. The fruit is seldom eaten raw but it can be used to make a good syrup and the juice is sometimes used to colour wine.

For freezing follow the instructions for freezing RASPBERRIES (page 139).

MUSHROOMS

Wild and cultivated mushrooms can be frozen successfully.

SELECTING FOR FREEZING

Only choose very fresh mushrooms for freezing. Leave small ones whole and slice larger ones.

PREPARATION FOR FREEZING

Do not wash, wipe with a damp clean cloth. Trim the end of the stalk and slice larger mushrooms. A little lemon juice will help to prevent discolouration.

TO FREEZE

Either fry in butter for 1-2 minutes (the preferred method), steam blanch for 3½ minutes or pack dry for short term storage. Cool quickly and pack, in usable quantities, in rigid containers. Leave a 2 cm/¾ inch headspace for blanched mushrooms. Seal, label and freeze.

STORAGE TIME: Raw for 1 month; cooked or blanched for 3 months.

TO DEFROST AND SERVE: Use fried, blanched and dry pack mushrooms from frozen. To cook, fry in butter for 5 minutes.

USES: Fried with grills; in soups and stews; as a filling for omelettes and flans; to make a savoury sauce for filling pancakes; in stuffings and made-up dishes.

MUSSELS

Mussels are an edible mollusc which has an elongated shell, blue black in colour with a slight roughness along the back. When bought the mussels should be closed, but they open naturally when cooked.

SELECTING FOR FREEZING

Choose specimens for freezing on the day of catching. Choose firm, unbroken mussels with a good amber flesh colour when opened.

PREPARATION FOR FREEZING

Boil and cool, then freeze as soon as possible. Boil and cool in the usual way. Open shells and remove the fish, retaining the juices. Wash the fish in salted water (using 30 ml/2 tablespoons salt to 600 ml/1 pint water) then drain thoroughly.

TO FREEZE

Pack fish and juices in usable quantities in rigid containers with crumpled greaseproof paper between the surface of the liquid and the lid.

STORAGE TIME: Up to 1 month.

TO DEFROST AND SERVE: Cook from frozen allowing very little extra cooking time or the fish will be tough.

USES: In salads, cold fish platters, steamed in wine with seasonings, baked in garlic butter and for adding to fish risottos and kedgeree-style mixtures.

MUTTON

Generally speaking one classes a lamb over 1 year old as mutton. The joints obtained are the same as for lamb but larger and the total carcass weight is greater. The meat is generally better cooked by slow-cooking methods.

For freezing follow the instructions for freezing LAMB (page 103).

NECTARINES

A nectarine has been described as a peach with a smooth, rather than hairy, rosy-red rather than peach, speckled skin.

SELECTING FOR FREEZING

Choose nectarines that are firm to the touch for freezing. They should have a good colour and not over-ripe or mushy feel.

PREPARATION FOR FREEZING

Skin if you like or wash the skins well. Cut in half, twist to separate the fruit, then remove the stone. Slice if you like but brush with lemon juice to prevent discolouration.

TO FREEZE

Pack the fruit in usable quantities in rigid containers, then cover with a medium sugar syrup (see page 25). Add 1.25 ml/¼ teaspoon ascorbic acid to 600 ml/1 pint of the syrup to prevent discolouration during the freezing process. Leave a 2 cm/¾ inch headspace, seal, label and freeze.

STORAGE TIME: Up to 12 months.

TO DEFROST AND SERVE: Defrost in the refrigerator for 3-4 hours.

USES: In fruit salads, flans and gâteaux or purée and use to make ice creams, fools, mousses and other whipped desserts. Nectarines also have a savoury use as they are delicious with ham, cheese and other cold, savoury dishes. Use at any time as a replacement for peaches.

OKRA

Also called 'lady's fingers' because of its shape and size, this green seed-filled pod is available in Britain in plentiful and cheap supplies in the summer months. It freezes well both raw and in made-up dishes.

SELECTING FOR FREEZING

Ideally choose small pods that are no longer than 5 cm/2 inches. Pods must be intact or the juices will run out during freezing.

PREPARATION FOR FREEZING

Trim the stems but do not puncture the pod.

TO FREEZE

Blanch the pods in boiling water for 3 minutes. Drain, cool quickly in iced water, drain again then pat dry with absorbent kitchen paper. Pack in usable quantities in rigid containers or polythene bags. Seal, label and freeze.

STORAGE TIME: Up to 12 months.

TO DEFROST AND SERVE: Cook from frozen in boiling water for about 6-8 minutes until tender. Alternatively, add to casseroles, curries, soups and made-up dishes of this nature while still frozen.

USES: Okra can be served as a vegetable accompaniment but is often better when mixed with hot spicy mixtures like curries. Also use in soups, casseroles and hot pots for interest, flavour and nutrition.

ONIONS

Onions are widely available, store well when fresh, so hardly merit a great deal of freezer space. They also require special attention in terms of packaging so that their flavours do not permeate everything else being stored.

SELECTING FOR FREEZING

Regardless of size from tiny bulb to fist-sized giant, onions should always feel firm to the touch. The skin should be dry, crisp and papery. Reject any on offer that show signs of mould, bruising or softness. Needless to say onions that are sprouting at the top are well beyond their peak.

PREPARATION FOR FREEZING

Trim at the top and tail and remove the skin. Grade for size. Small onions can be frozen whole, larger ones can be sliced or chopped.

TO FREEZE

Whole button onions and shallots should be blanched in boiling water for 2-4 minutes, depending upon size. Drain, cool quickly in iced water, drain again and pat dry with absorbent kitchen paper. Pack in usable quantities in polythene bags. Seal very well (overwrapping if necessary), label and freeze. Sliced and chopped onions should be blanched in boiling water for 1 minute for chopped onions and 2 minutes for sliced. Drain, cool quickly in iced water, drain again and pat dry with absorbent kitchen paper. Pack in usable quantities in polythene bags and overwrap again. Seal, label and freeze.

STORAGE TIME: Up to 6 months.

TO DEFROST AND SERVE: Leave whole onions to defrost in their wrappings for 2 hours at room temperature. Alternatively add while still frozen to casseroles and sauces and adjust the cooking time accordingly. Use sliced and chopped onions where fresh onions would be required or leave to stand in their wrappings at room temperature for 1 hour to defrost before using.

USES: Onions have countless uses and frozen onions can be used wherever fresh are. Consider them in soups, sauces, casseroles, hot pots, gratins, sautéed dishes, stir-fries, as fried onions to accompany grills and as a vegetable accompaniment when mixed with other vegetables like peas, sweetcorn, peppers and mushrooms.

ORANGES

One variety of orange or another is available during every month of the year so you are hardly likely to freeze them due to unavailability. It is possible however that you may have a preference for a particular type or that you are faced with an unbelievable bargain and want to consider freezing oranges for eating in the future.

PREPARATION FOR FREEZING

Grate the rind finely or remove the skin thinly with a canelle knife or vegetable peeler. Cut into thin julienne strips if you like. Remove the remaining rind and pith then slice across into rings or cut into segments.

TO FREEZE

Wrap usable amounts of grated or sliced peel in foil or cling film. Seal, label and freeze. Open freeze slices or segments of orange until solid then place in usable quantities in rigid containers, sprinkling with a little sugar if you like. Seal, label and return to the freezer. Alternatively, cover with a light sugar syrup (see page 25), seal, label and freeze.

STORAGE TIME: Up to 12 months.

TO DEFROST AND SERVE: Unwrap parcels of rind and leave to stand at room temperature for about 5 minutes to defrost sufficiently to use. Leave slices and segments in their containers and defrost at room temperature for about 1 hour, then use as for fresh oranges.

USES: Rind can be used as a flavouring, garnish or decoration. Orange slices and segments can be used for making desserts and marmalade.

OYSTERS

The oyster is a bivalve mollusc which lives in shallow waters and is in season from September until April. The best are called Natives, which are cultivated round the Kent and Essex coasts of England, particularly Whitstable and Colchester. Oysters are considered very nutritious and are generally eaten raw with a little lemon juice and cayenne pepper. They can however be cooked and a favourite way of serving them is wrapped in bacon as Angels on Horseback.

For freezing follow the instructions for freezing MUSSELS (page 114).

To serve raw, thaw in the container in the refrigerator until completely defrosted then eat as soon as possible.

PANCAKES

Pancakes freeze very well. To prevent them from becoming rubbery during freezing, add 15 ml/1 tablespoon of oil to the basic recipe. Pancakes can be frozen filled or unfilled:

UNFILLED PANCAKES

PREPARATION AND TO FREEZE

Pancakes must be cold before packing: to cool quickly and to allow the steam to escape, slip cooled pancakes onto a wire cooling tray. If you want to remove only a few pancakes at a time then interleave them. Seal tightly in stacks, in polythene bags, or wrapped in foil if foil is to be used for reheating. Label and freeze.

STORAGE TIME: Up to 6 months.

TO DEFROST AND SERVE: Leave in the packaging at room temperature for 2-3 hours, or overnight in the refrigerator. For rapid defrosting, unwrap, spread out singly and leave at room temperature for 15-20 minutes.
   To reheat, place a stack (4-5 pancakes) of frozen pancakes, wrapped in foil, in a moderately hot oven, 200°C/400°F/Gas 6, for 20-30 minutes, or heat individual pancakes in a lightly greased frying pan, about 30 seconds on each side.

FILLED PANCAKES

PREPARATION AND TO FREEZE

Pancakes filled with a sweet or savoury filling freeze well, provided the fillings also freeze well, eg avoid fillings containing hard-boiled eggs and sliced tomato as a garnish. Remember also not to over-season savoury fillings. Pack the cooled and filled pancakes in a greased foil dish and seal with heavy-duty foil. Label and freeze.
   Alternatively, the fillings and pancakes can be frozen separately and assembled after defrosting.

STORAGE TIME: Up to 2-4 months, depending upon the filling.

TO DEFROST AND SERVE: Place frozen, in the packaging, in a moderately hot oven, 200°C/400°F/Gas 6 for 30 minutes.

PAPAYAS

Papayas or pawpaws are tropical fruit, similar in size to mangoes. The skin of the papaya is thin and smooth, green when underipe and yellow when ripe. The flesh varies from yellow to orange and is sweet tasting.

SELECTING FOR FREEZING

Look for bargains in the spring months. Choose fresh, unblemished specimens.

PREPARATION FOR FREEZING

Peel, cut in half lengthways and scoop out the black seeds. Cut the flesh into thin slices.

TO FREEZE

Freeze in a sugar syrup pack or as a purée. For a sugar syrup pack, pack usable quantities of papaya slices in rigid containers, then cover with a medium sugar syrup (see page 25) to which 10 ml/2 teaspoons lemon juice has been added for every 600 ml/1 pint syrup. Leave a 2 cm/¾ inch headspace. Seal, label and freeze.

To make a purée, place the papaya slices in a blender or food processor and purée until smooth. Pour, in usable quantities, into rigid containers. Leave a 2 cm/¾ inch headspace. Seal, label and freeze.

STORAGE TIME: Up to 6 months.

TO DEFROST AND SERVE: Defrost sugar syrup packs in their container at room temperature for 1-2 hours. Defrost papaya purée in the refrigerator overnight.

USES: Use sugar syrup pack papayas in fruit salads and wherever peaches and apricots might be used. Use papaya purée for making ice creams, sorbets, soufflés and mousses.

PARSNIPS

Parsnips store well in the ground so unless you are buying a bargain, kitchen gardeners are advised to leave them naturally in the soil. In fact they taste better after there has been a frost.

SELECTION FOR FREEZING

Select small, young and fresh parsnips. Only freeze if you have plenty of available freezer space.

PREPARATION FOR FREEZING

Remove the tops, wash, peel thinly then slice into thin discs.

TO FREEZE

Blanch in boiling water for 2 minutes, drain, cool in iced water, drain again and pat dry with absorbent kitchen paper. Pack, in usable quantities in polythene bags, seal, label and freeze. Parsnips added to other vegetables in a stew pack need not be blanched for short storage times.

Alternatively, cook as usual and purée in a blender or food processor. Spoon into rigid containers, in usable quantities, leaving a 2 cm/¾ inch headspace. Seal, label and freeze.

STORAGE TIME: 9-12 months for blanched parsnips; 8-10 months for parsnip purée; and up to 3 months for a stew pack.

TO DEFROST AND SERVE: Cook from frozen except for the purée. Cook in boiling water for 8-12 minutes. Defrost the purée in the container at room temperature for 2-3 hours. Reheat gently until hot to use.

USES: In soups, stews and casseroles.

PARTRIDGES

There are two main varieties of this small game bird; the European Grey and the slightly larger French red-legged partridge, sometimes found in the eastern counties of Britain. The grey partridge is considered best for table use and is generally served plainly roasted. The red-legged partridge is at its prime when mature and so is excellent braised or casseroled. The partridge season is from September to January.

For freezing follow the instructions for freezing PHEASANTS (see page 128).

PASSIONFRUIT

This small brownish fruit is a native of South America and Australia and is imported during the spring and summer months.

SELECTING FOR FREEZING

Look for passionfruit where the skin is soft and slightly wrinkled and purple in colour. The fruit should feel heavy for its size.

PREPARATION FOR FREEZING

Cut the fruit in half and scoop out the pulp with the seeds.

TO FREEZE

Weigh the pulp and mix with half its weight of sugar. Stir well and leave until the sugar has completely dissolved. Spoon, in usable quantities, into rigid containers, leaving a 2 cm/¾ inch headspace. Seal, label and freeze.

STORAGE TIME: Up to 12 months.

TO DEFROST AND SERVE: Thaw in the covered container at room temperature for about 1½ hours.

USES: Stir well then spoon over ice cream or use in fruit salads. Alternatively spoon over cheesecakes as a topping or use to fill a meringue-type dessert like pavlova along with whipped cream.

PASTA

This covers all items like spaghetti, macaroni, noodles, lasagne etc. Although the latter take very little time to cook from fresh, it may be useful to store cooked pasta in the freezer for a special party or to freeze away leftovers for salads and other made-up dishes.

PREPARATION FOR FREEZING
Slightly undercook the pasta if cooking especially for the freezer. Cool under cold running water, drain well and pat dry with absorbent kitchen paper.

TO FREEZE
Pack, in usable quantities, in polythene bags. Seal, label and freeze.

STORAGE TIME: 2 months.

TO DEFROST AND SERVE: Add from frozen to boiling water and simmer until *al dente* or just tender. Drain to serve.

USES: As a main meal accompaniment with butter and seasonings. Use to make pasta salads, made-up layered pasta dishes like lasagne and cannelloni and to add to soups to make them more substantial.

PASTRY

CHOUX PASTRY

For making sweet and savoury eclairs, profiteroles and cream buns.
Freeze either baked or unbaked.

PREPARATION AND TO FREEZE

The raw uncooked pastry can be frozen in bulk but it is best shaped
before freezing as the frozen shapes can be baked while still frozen. Pack
bulk choux pastry in a rigid container. Seal, label and freeze.

Pipe or spoon choux pastry onto a baking sheet and open freeze until
solid. Pack, in usable quantities, in polythene bags, seal, label and return
to the freezer.

Baked choux shapes can be frozen after baking. Cool quickly, pack in
bags or foil. Seal, label and freeze.

STORAGE TIME: Up to 3 months.

TO DEFROST AND SERVE: Leave choux pastry frozen in bulk at
room temperature for 3-4 hours to defrost or overnight in the
refrigerator. Use as normal fresh choux pastry.

Bake frozen shaped but raw choux pastry shapes in a moderately hot
oven (200°C/400°F/Gas 6) according to the recipe instructions but
allowing 5 minutes extra cooking time.

Defrost baked choux pastry shapes at room temperature for about 1
hour, then remove wrappings and refresh in a moderate oven
(180°C/350°F/Gas 4) for 5 minutes, or unwrap and place while still
frozen in a moderate oven for 10 minutes.

FLAKY PASTRY

Ideally freeze flaky pastry in its raw state.

PREPARATION AND TO FREEZE

Prepare bulk quantities of flaky pastry up to the last rolling. Pack in
polythene bags or heavy-duty foil. Seal, label and freeze.

Flaky pastry pies – freeze as for Shortcrust Pastry Pies (see page 123).

Flaky pastry pie lids – freeze as for Shortcrust Pastry Pie Lids
(see page 123).

Vol-au-vent cases – see VOL-AU-VENTS (page 169)

STORAGE TIME: 6 months.

TO DEFROST AND SERVE: Defrost bulk flaky pastry for 3-4 hours at
room temperature or thaw overnight in the refrigerator.

For pies - unwrap and place frozen in the oven. Bake flaky pastry at

220°C/425°F/Gas 7 for 25 minutes. Bake Puff Pastry at 230°C/450°F/Gas 8 for 15-20 minutes. Reduce both oven temperatures to 190°C/375°F/Gas 5, if the filling requires longer cooking.

For pie lids - dampen the edge of the filled pie dish and place the frozen lid on top. Bake as above for pies.

If pies are frozen with a baked flaky pastry topping then defrost at room temperature for 2-4 hours depending upon size. Reheat if required.

PUFF PASTRY

For freezing follow the instructions for freezing FLAKY PASTRY (page 122).

SHORTCRUST PASTRY

If shortcrust pastry is frozen in bulk it takes 3 hours at room temperature to thaw before it can be rolled so there is little advantage to freezing it in this way. Ideally shape into pies, flan cases, tartlets or pie lids before freezing unbaked or baked.

UNBAKED
PREPARATION AND TO FREEZE

PIES – make large pies in foil dishes or plates; make small pies in patty tins or foil dishes. Do not make a steam vent in the lid. Open freeze until solid. When frozen, leave large and small pies in foil dishes and overwrap with foil. Remove small pies from patty tins and pack in heavy-duty foil or polythene bags. Seal, label and freeze.

PIE LIDS – prepare in quantity and cut into shape to fit pie dish. Open freeze until solid. Pack several together interleaving with foil inside a rigid container. Seal, label and freeze.

FLAN CASES – freeze in flan ring or foil case until solid, remove ring or case, wrap in a polythene bag or heavy-duty foil, then pack in a box for protection. Seal, label and freeze.

TARTLET CASES – freeze uncovered in patty tins; when solid remove from tins; pack in polythene or heavy-duty foil then pack into a box for added protection. Seal, label and freeze.

STORAGE TIME: 6 months.

TO DEFROST AND SERVE:

PIES – unwrap and place in a preheated oven and bake as usual, allowing a little extra time for defrosting. Cut a vent in the pastry lid as the pie begins to thaw.

❄ FLAN CASES – unpack and place frozen case into flan ring on a baking sheet. Bake 'blind' at 200°C/400°F/Gas 6, for 20-25 minutes.

TARTLET CASES – unpack and place frozen into patty tins and bake at 200°C/400°F/Gas 6, for about 15 minutes.

PIE LIDS – dampen edge of filled pie dish and place lid on top, bake at 200°C/400°F/Gas 6 for 20-25 minutes, reduce oven to 150°C/300°F/Gas 2 for a further 10-15 minutes.

——— BAKED ———
PREPARATION AND TO FREEZE

PIES – bake in foil dishes or plates. Cool quickly and pack in heavy-duty foil. Seal, label and freeze.

FLAN AND TARTLET CASES – pack cooled cases in polythene containers or foil and then a box for added protection. Seal, label and freeze.

STORAGE TIME: Meat pies 3-4 months; fruit pies up to 6 months; unfilled cases up to 6 months.

TO DEFROST AND SERVE:
PIES – leave at room temperature for 2-4 hours, depending upon the size of the pie. Reheat in the oven if required hot.

FLAN AND TARTLET CASES – leave at room temperature for about 1 hour.

——— SUET PASTRY ———

As suet pastry is quick and easy to make there is no advantage to be gained from freezing it in bulk. Savoury or sweet puddings can be frozen uncooked or cooked and then placed straight from the freezer into the steamer. Uncooked puddings of the steak and kidney type require a cooking time of about 5 hours and so are best frozen in their cooked state. Remember not to over-season savoury fillings.

PREPARATION AND TO FREEZE

Make up cooked puddings in foil or polythene basins and cook as per the recipe instructions. Cool quickly, wrap the basin tightly in foil, seal, label and freeze.

STORAGE TIME: Up to 3 months.

TO DEFROST AND SERVE: Remove the wrapping and cover the top with foil or a polythene lid and place, still frozen, in a steamer. A 1 kg/2 lb size steak and kidney pudding takes about 3 hours to reheat; and a fruit pudding about 2½ hours. Times will be less if you use a pressure cooker.

PÂTÉS

All pâté freezes well – although coarse ones with a good deal of fat have a slightly shorter storage life than the smooth type. High alcohol content also slightly shortens storage life and it should be remembered that seasonings and spices intensify on freezing and the recipe may need a little adjustment.

If making pâté in a terrine dish or loaf dish, when chilled 'firm but not solid' slice through into portion sizes. In this way, individual portions may be removed. It will also decrease defrosting time of the whole if necessary.

STORAGE TIME: Very much dependent upon the content but as an approximate guide 2-3 months, 1 month if including bacon.

TO DEFROST AND SERVE: Ideally defrost in the refrigerator overnight, or if needed faster, at room temperature for 2-4 hours.

PEAS

It is only worth freezing your own home-grown fresh peas since those available in the shops are already so much older than commercially frozen ones (and whose flavour and tenderness are hard to match never mind beat).

SELECTING FOR FREEZING
Choose young, tender, sweet peas with crisp, green shells.

PREPARATION FOR FREEZING
Pod but there is no need to wash.

TO FREEZE
Blanch in boiling water for 1-1½ minutes, depending upon size. Drain, cool in iced water, drain again and pat dry with absorbent kitchen paper. Pack, in usable quantities, in polythene bags. Seal, label and freeze.

STORAGE TIME: 12 months.

TO DEFROST AND SERVE: Cook from frozen in boiling water for 5-8 minutes.

USES: Hot as a vegetable, for use in soups, vegetable mixtures, casseroles, stir-fries and chilled in summer salads with a minty dressing.

PEACHES

Prepare and freeze as for nectarines, their close cousins, but ideally skin first.

For freezing follow the instructions for freezing NECTARINES (page 114).

PEARS

Strong-flavoured pears like Conference, Williams and Comice are ideal for freezing.

SELECTING FOR FREEZING
Choose strong-flavoured pears that are ripe but not soft.

PREPARATION FOR FREEZING
Peel, core and slice. Cook in a medium sugar syrup (see page 25) for 1-1½ minutes. Add a little lemon juice or ascorbic acid to prevent discolouration. Cool quickly, pack in usable quantities into rigid containers, allowing a 2 cm/¾ inch headspace. Seal, label and freeze.

STORAGE TIME: 8 months.

TO DEFROST AND SERVE: Release from packaging and place in a pan. Stew gently from frozen until cooked. Serve warm or allow to cool then chill.

USES: In fruit salads, in tarts, flans and other made-up fruit puddings.

PEPPERS

Peppers may be frozen for use in cooked dishes but sadly lose too much of their crisp texture to be used in salads after freezing.

SELECTING FOR FREEZING

All pepper colours including green, orange, red, yellow and black can be frozen. Look for firm, glossy specimens at their peak in July and August.

PREPARATION FOR FREEZING

Remove the stalks and deseed.

TO FREEZE

Peppers do not need to be blanched for short term storage. Leave whole for easy stuffing or halve, slice or dice as desired. For longer storage blanch in boiling water for 2-3 minutes, depending upon size. Drain, cool in iced water, drain again and pat dry with absorbent kitchen paper. Pack in usable quantities in polythene bags. Seal, label and freeze.

STORAGE TIME: Unblanched up to 2 months; blanched 9-12 months; stuffed peppers take the storage time of the stuffing as a guide.

TO DEFROST AND SERVE: Cook from frozen, including stuffed peppers.

USES: In vegetable mixtures, cooked salad mixtures, stews, casseroles, pies, quiches and made-up dishes.

PERSIMMONS

The persimmon is a soft fruit with a pleasantly tart flavour, not unlike a tomato but has a yellowish, orange colour. It is imported from the Mediterranean and southern states of America. Look out for ripe fruit in July and August.

SELECTING FOR FREEZING

Choose firm but ripe fruit with no signs of bruising.

PREPARATION FOR FREEZING

To prepare the whole fruit, peel off the skins. Leave whole or cut into slices.

TO FREEZE

Wrap individual whole fruit in foil. Seal, label and freeze.
   Pack slices, in usable quantities, in rigid containers and cover with a heavy sugar syrup (see page 25). Leave a 2 cm/¾ inch headspace. Seal, label and freeze.

STORAGE TIME: Whole persimmons up to 2 months; sliced in sugar syrup up to 12 months.

TO DEFROST AND SERVE: Leave whole persimmons to defrost in their wrappings at room temperature for 3 hours.
Defrost sliced persimmons in the same way.

USES: Whole persimmons can be served with cream or ice cream; sliced persimmons can be served the same way or added to fruit salad mixtures or other fruit desserts for added interest.

PET FOODS

Every care must be taken when freezing pet foods, as the standards of hygiene in handling are not usually as rigid as those laid down in the production of food for human consumption, so there could be a risk of cross-contamination between this and the other food in your freezer.

Therefore, it is essential that all pet food is kept in an entirely separate section in the freezer. Pet foods can be frozen either in the raw state or cooked.

PREPARATION AND TO FREEZE

Divide into usable quantities and pack into polythene bags. Seal, label clearly and freeze.

STORAGE TIME: As pet foods normally consist of cheaper cuts of meat and offal and fish that is probably not quite as fresh as we would like it to be for human consumption, the storage life is only 3 months. After this time there is rapid deterioration in quality.

PHEASANTS

Pheasants are small game birds in season during the winter months from October. They are usually sold in pairs as a brace. The hen bird, which is the smaller of the two and whose plumage is less brilliant in colour, is considered to have the finer flavour. The average weight when prepared is about 1 kg/2¼ lbs.

SELECTING FOR FREEZING

Pheasants are considered at their best before 15 months old. Buy birds from a good quality supplier and check for lead shot. Farm-reared birds are also available oven-ready, fresh or frozen.

PREPARATION FOR FREEZING

Hang if necessary, then pluck, draw and wash thoroughly inside and out. Dry then truss if necessary. Do not stuff. Reserve giblets separately, discarding the sac from the gizzard.

TO FREEZE

Pad protruding bones with foil, then wrap whole birds individually with foil and overwrap in polythene bags. If the game is very high then use several bags and seal each one tightly. Pack giblets in rigid containers, keeping livers separate for use in pâtés etc. Seal, label and freeze.

STORAGE TIME: Up to 6 months, 3 months for the giblets.

TO DEFROST AND SERVE: Pheasants must be throughly thawed before cooking and must be cooked immediately after defrosting. Thaw in the wrappings in the refrigerator for up to 24 hours, according to size. Thaw giblets in the container in the refrigerator for about 12 hours.

USES: Pheasant are probably best roasted but older birds can be casseroled.

PIES

For freezing follow the instructions for freezing PASTRY (page 122-124).

PIGEONS

Pigeons are only acceptable for freezing and cooking when young. They are generally available all year round but are at their best from August to October. They can be roasted, sautéed, grilled or stewed.

For freezing follow the instructions for freezing WOODCOCK (see page 171) but defrost in their wrappings in the refrigerator for up to 24 hours, according to size.

PINEAPPLES

Pineapples are available all year round but occasionally they can be found at very good prices – this is the time to freeze a few away for enjoyment at a later date.

SELECTING FOR FREEZING

Look out for bargains where the price may be reduced due to imperfections of the skin. Since this is cut away it will not affect the eating or freezing quality of the pineapple.

PREPARATION FOR FREEZING

Peel, core and remove the eyes. Cut into slices or chunks.

TO FREEZE

Pack the fruit, in rigid containers sprinkling sugar between each layer and allowing 225 g/8 oz sugar to every 450 g/1 lb fruit. Seal, label and freeze.
  Alternatively, pack in rigid containers and cover with a heavy sugar syrup (see page 25). Leave a 2 cm/¾ inch headspace. Seal, label and freeze.

STORAGE TIME: 9-12 months.

TO DEFROST AND SERVE: Defrost both sugar and syrup packs slowly in the refrigerator, preferably overnight.

USES: As a dessert with cream or ice cream, sprinkled with liqueur like Kirsch if desired; in fruit salads, crumble mixtures and mixed fruit pies and tarts.

PIZZAS

Pizzas can be frozen either baked or unbaked.

PREPARATION FOR FREEZING

If preparing unbaked pizzas then use cooked or canned tomatoes for the topping, as fresh tomato slices do not freeze well and are watery on consequent baking. Prepare to the baking stage. To prepare baked pizzas, bake according to the recipe and allow to cool.

TO FREEZE

Wrap unbaked and cooled baked pizzas in heavy-duty foil or polythene. Seal, label and freeze.

STORAGE TIME: Baked pizzas for up to 1 month; unbaked pizzas up to 2 months.

TO DEFROST AND SERVE: To defrost and cook baked pizzas, remove the packaging and place frozen in a cold oven set at 230°C/450°F/Gas 8. Turn on the oven and bake for 30-35 minutes.
  To defrost unbaked pizzas, remove the packaging and place frozen in a moderately hot oven, 200°C/400°F, Gas 6 for 20 minutes, or leave in the packaging at room temperature for 2 hours before baking for 10-15 minutes.

PLAICE

Plaice is a flat sea-water fish that is available all year round but considered at its best from May to December. It can be fried, grilled or baked either in fillets or whole. The flesh is rather fragile and for that reason, bought fillets always have the skin left on one side. Plaice is easily distinguisable by the orange or red spots on the dark upper side. For freezing follow the instructions for freezing COD (see page 69).

PLUMS

All plums and gages can be frozen successfully in a sugar syrup solution.

SELECTING FOR FREEZING
Select ripe but firm fruit with unblemished skins.

PREPARATION FOR FREEZING
Halve and stone, skin if feasible.

TO FREEZE
Pack, in usable quantities, in rigid containers and cover with a heavy sugar syrup (see page 25). Leave a 2 cm/¾ inch headspace. Seal, label and freeze. Add a little lemon juice or ascorbic acid to the syrup to prevent discolouration if you like.

Whole plums that have been washed and dried can also be frozen whole, complete with their stones. Pack in polythene bags. Seal, label and freeze.

STORAGE TIME: 6 months.

TO DEFROST AND SERVE: Defrost at room temperature for about 3-4 hours. Alternatively, use from frozen in pies, crumbles or other dishes requiring cooked plums.

Whole frozen plums should be defrosted in the refrigerator overnight and used as for fresh plums.

USES: In pies, crumbles, flans, sauces and as a stewed fruit dessert. Whole defrosted plums can be used for both sweets and savouries and to make jams and other preserves

POMEGRANATES

Since pomegranates are only available from September to December it is worthwhile storing a few in the freezer, especially when there is a glut and prices are good.

PREPARATION AND TO FREEZE

Cut in half and scoop out the juicy seeds, discarding any membrane. Pack into rigid containers and cover with a medium sugar syrup (see page 25). As the juice is the best part of the fruit this can be extracted by rubbing the seeds through a sieve. Freeze down the juice in ice cube trays and when solid transfer to polythene bags. Seal, label and freeze.

STORAGE TIME: 12 months.

TO DEFROST AND SERVE: Defrost in the container at room temperature for 2 hours. The juice can be defrosted until liquid, about 1-2 hours.

USES: Use the fruit in fruit salads or serve on their own with a little lemon juice added, or with ice cream; the juice can make a refreshing drink.

PORK

A full pig carcase weighs about 36-45 kg/80-120 lbs, taking up about 77-112 litres/2¾-4 cu ft of freezer space. This may well prove to be too much for a small freezer owner, so a side of pork is a more popular buy to cut up and freeze.

SELECTING FOR FREEZING

It is possible to buy pork at any time of the year and there is no real seasonal fluctuation, although as demand falls in the summer the price does tend to drop a little. Cuts obtained are leg, which can be cut into 2-3 joints, chump end, loin, tenderloin, loin chops, belly, shoulder, hand, spring, trotters and head. Do ask your butcher if he will score the rind on the joints for you.

Joints will come from the leg (which can be left whole but are usually cut into the fillet end and the knuckle end); the loin (sold on the bone or boned, rolled and tied, and divided into the foreloin, middle loin and chump ends); belly (sold on and off the bone and divided into thick and streaky ends); shoulder or neck end (including sparerib and blade and can be boned and rolled); and the hand and spring (where the hand can be boned and rolled).

Chops, steaks, escalopes, rashers and spareribs can come from the following: the leg fillet, eye of loin and tenderloin where the meat is cut into thin slices or escalopes; the loin is usually divided into foreloin chops from the rib or neck end, middle loin chops and chump chops; the belly is cut into rashers or boned to provide spareribs; the shoulder can also be cut into sparerib chops.

Boneless cubes of pork come from leg, tenderloin, shoulder and hand. Minced pork will invariably come from boneless meat from the shoulder.

PREPARATION FOR FREEZING AND TO FREEZE

JOINTS (for roasting/pot roasting): Saw off any protruding bone ends and remove surplus fat. Leave skin on for crackling if you like. Pad bones with foil. Roll and tie boneless meat if not already done by the butcher, but do not stuff. Pork crown roast can be made by tying 2 foreloins together. Wrap individual joints in cling film or foil, then overwrap in a polythene bag. Exclude as much air as possible. Seal, label and freeze.

CHOPS, STEAKS, ESCALOPES, RASHERS AND SPARERIBS (for grilling/frying/roasting/barbecuing): Trim off bone ends and surplus fat. Leave skin on for crackling if you like. Pad bones with foil. Wrap individually in cling film or interleave, then pack together in polythene bags. Exclude as much air as possible. Seal, label and freeze.

CUBES (for casseroling/pies/sautéeing/stews): Trim off surplus fat, sinews and gristle. Cut boneless meat into 2.5 cm/1 inch cubes if not already cut. Pack cubes in usable quantities in polythene bags. Exclude as much air as possible. Seal, label and freeze.

MINCED PORK: Leave loose or shape into burgers, meatballs, patties etc. Pack loose mince in usable quantities in polythene bags. Exclude as much air as possible. Seal, label and freeze. To freeze burgers, meatballs and patties see BURGERS (page 50).

STORAGE TIME: Joints other than belly for up to 9 months; belly joints for up to 6 months; chops, steaks, rashers, escalopes and spareribs other than belly up to 9 months (those from the belly 6 months); cubes for up to 9 months; and minced pork for up to 3 months.

TO DEFROST AND SERVE

JOINTS: Defrost in the wrappings at room temperature for 6-8 hours per kg/3-4 hours per lb, then cook as for fresh until 87°C/190°F is registered on a meat thermometer. Never cook pork joints from frozen.

CHOPS, STEAKS, ESCALOPES, RASHERS AND SPARERIBS: Defrost in their wrappings at room temperature for 2-3 hours or in a refrigerator overnight, then cook as fresh. Alternatively, grill or fry from frozen, allowing extra time and brushing liberally with oil.

CUBES: Defrost in their wrappings at room temperature until pieces separate, then cook as for fresh, allowing a little extra time and using the thawed juices.

MINCED PORK: Partially defrost loose mince in its wrappings in the refrigerator, then cook as for fresh, stirring well to prevent sticking. Cook burgers, meatballs etc, from frozen.

USES: Like beef and lamb, pork is a versatile meat that can be roasted, pot-roasted, grilled, fried, barbecued, casseroled, sautéed, stewed, stir-fried and baked in a multitude of ways. It is also good for making pâtés and savoury terrines and the head for making brawn.

POTATOES

Potatoes, in various guises, can be frozen. Follow the guidelines below for success:

SELECTING FOR FREEZING:

NEW: Choose small, new, even-sized potatoes. Freeze only if direct from grower and plenty of freezer space is available. Ideal for special 'out of season' eating.

CHIPS: See *Chips* (page 66).

ROAST: Consider roasting extra when you are cooking a batch and freeze the surplus to immediate requirements.

DUCHESSE: Worth piping a few for special occasions.

CROQUETTES: Better bought commercially.

JACKET POTATOES: Not as good as freshly baked, but useful for party preparation if they have been prepared with a filling (cheese, tuna etc); otherwise they may just as well be prepared fresh since there is no saving on time or effort.

CRISPS, BOILED AND CREAMED POTATOES: Not really worthwhile in terms of saving time or effort.

PREPARATION FOR FREEZING

All as for fresh; all the above cooked before freezing, except new potatoes. Slightly undercook these with or without the skins. Drain, toss in a little butter, then pack in boil-in-bags (with perhaps a sprig of fresh mint). Alternatively blanch in boiling water for 2 minutes. Drain, cool in iced water, drain again and pat dry with absorbent kitchen paper. Pack, in usable quantities in polythene bags. Seal, label and freeze.

TO FREEZE

Cool all types in the refrigerator then open freeze on trays until solid.

Pack, in usable quantities, in polythene bags or rigid containers. Wrap solid-baked jacket potatoes in foil. Seal, label and freeze.

STORAGE TIME: Blanched new potatoes up to 12 months; cooked potatoes of all types up to 3 months.

TO DEFROST AND SERVE

NEW: Cook small ones from frozen, larger ones defrost for better judgement of reheating times. Cook small ones in boiling water or butter for 5-10 minutes.

ROAST POTATOES: Best cooked from frozen. May be reheated in a hot oven but best results are when deep-fat fried.

DUCHESSE: Best cooked from frozen, heat through and cook in a very hot oven for only a few minutes.

CROQUETTES: May be cooked from frozen; avoid too hot a fat for frying. Deep fry until hot and an even golden colour.

JACKET: Cook from frozen in a cool to warm oven. Keep wrapped in their foil covering and allow 1-2 hours.

POUSSINS

See *Chickens* (page 62)

PRAWNS

There are several varieties of this crustacean, which is mainly found in the Mediterranean and the Atlantic. The English prawn is caught around most coasts and is smaller than the Mediterranean or Pacific prawn. Dublin Bay prawns, called scampi when shelled, are a different variety with a harder shell.

SELECTING FOR FREEZING

Most prawns sold are ready cooked but some are available, like Tiger Prawns, raw. Look for cooked prawns with a firm-textured flesh and bright pink colour. Check that they have not been frozen previously. Raw prawns will still be a greyish colour and should be plump and fresh and have a clean smell.

PREPARATION FOR FREEZING

Freeze on the day of purchase or catching as soon as possible after boiling and cooling in the usual way. Twist off the heads leaving the tails in the shell. Wash in salted water (using 30 ml/2 tablespoons salt to 600 ml/1 pint water), then drain thoroughly. Prawns ideally should be cooked in boiling salted water for 2-4 minutes then drained and cooled before freezing.

TO FREEZE
Pack in usable quantities in polythene bags. Seal, label and freeze.

STORAGE TIME: Up to 1 month.

TO DEFROST AND SERVE: Cook raw prawns from frozen allowing very little extra cooking time or they will become tough. Cooked prawns should be defrosted in their wrappings in the refrigerator for 2-3 hours then served cold or used in dishes where they are further cooked for the minimum amount of time.

USES: Prawns can be boiled, steamed or grilled and added cooked and cold to salads. They can also be added to rice and pasta dishes, used to make sandwich fillings, to fill flans, quiches and pastries like vol-au-vents and served as part of a cold buffet with dips and sauces.

PUMPKINS

Pumpkins store well in a cool, dry, frost-free place. Freezing is only recommended and worthwhile if ready prepared pumpkin is required at short notice or for out-of-season eating.

SELECTING FOR FREEZING
Look out for bargains in September and October. Choose small and medium-sized specimens.

PREPARATION FOR FREEZING
Wash, peel and cut in half. Remove the seeds and strings and cut into slices or cubes. Steam, bake or boil in a little water until tender. Drain, leave in slices or mash.

TO FREEZE
Cool quickly, pack into rigid containers, leaving a 2 cm/¾ inch headspace. Seal, label and freeze.

STORAGE TIME: 12 months.

TO DEFROST AND SERVE: Reheat from frozen, preferably in a double boiler. Or thaw in the container at room temperature for about 2 hours for use in pies etc.

USES: For making pumpkin pie; to serve as a vegetable accompaniment; in sweet and savoury pies and for mashed potato and pumpkin toppings.

QUAILS

Quails are bred in this country from stock imported from Malaya and are sold all the year round, though they are in prime condition from September to January. Quail should be plump and firm and they are often cooked undrawn. They should not be allowed to get high. They are excellent spatchcocked or can be roasted whole. A vine leaf is often tucked underneath the barding. Allow at least one bird per person.

For freezing follow the instructions for freezing WOODCOCK (see page 171) drawing the bird if you like before freezing.

QUICHES

Best results are obtained for quiches that are completely baked.

PREPARATION FOR FREEZING
Bake as per recipe instructions but remember to brush the base with egg white before adding the filling – this helps to keep the pastry base crisp. Allow to cool completely.

TO FREEZE
Open freeze until solid. Wrap in heavy-duty foil or polythene. Seal, label and freeze.

STORAGE TIME: 4-6 months.

TO DEFROST AND SERVE: If a flan ring has been used then replace the ring for reheating. Reheat from frozen in a warm oven, 180°C/350°F/Gas 4, for about 25-30 minutes.

RABBITS

The rabbit is a small rodent of the hare family and, like the hare, is classed as game.

SELECTING FOR FREEZING
There are basically two kinds of rabbit, the tame or Ostend rabbit, and wild rabbit. Tame rabbits, bred and fattened for the table, are larger and have a more delicate flesh than the wild ones. They are also much larger

and can weigh up to 4 kg/9 lbs while the ordinary wild rabbit seldom weighs more than 1.4 kg/3 lbs. Unlike poultry, which is plucked and hung without being drawn, rabbits should be paunched as soon as they are killed and then hung with the skin still on. The meat of rabbits is generally very tender, not unlike chicken and they do not necessarily need to be hung before eating.

PREPARATION FOR FREEZING
Hang if necessary, skin and wash inside and out in lightly salted water. Dry thoroughly with absorbent kitchen paper, then leave whole or halve as you like.

TO FREEZE
Pad any protruding bones with foil, then wrap individually with foil and overwrap in polythene bags. Seal, label and freeze.

STORAGE TIME: Up to 6 months.

TO DEFROST AND SERVE: Defrost at room temperature for up to 18 hours depending upon size.

USES: A young rabbit can be roasted plainly or stuffed and then roasted. Older rabbits are better casseroled or used in stews.

RADISHES, SUMMER

Like most salad vegetables, radishes do not freeze successfully, as they lose their crispness and flavour upon defrosting.

RADISHES, WINTER

Unlike its summer counterpart the winter radish can be frozen most successfully.

SELECTING FOR FREEZING
Choose firm, undamaged roots without blemishes that are about 30 cm/12 inches long with a good black skin. For easy preparation choose roots that have very few side shoots. If the leaves are still attached they should be crisp and bright green; reject any that are limp. They are generally available in the shops from October.

PREPARATION FOR FREEZING
Trim the roots and wash thoroughly, scrubbing well to remove any dirt. Peel thinly with a sharp knife then grate or dice as you like.

TO FREEZE

Pack grated winter radish in usable quantities in polythene bags then seal, label and freeze. Blanch diced winter radish in boiling water for 2 minutes. Cool rapidly in iced water, drain and pat dry with absorbent kitchen paper. Pack in usable quantities in polythene bags. Seal, label and freeze.

STORAGE TIME: Up to 6 months.

TO DEFROST AND SERVE: Leave grated winter radish to defrost in its wrappings at room temperature for 3 hours. Pat dry with absorbent kitchen paper before serving. Cook diced winter radish from frozen in boiling salted water for about 8 minutes or until tender. Drain and serve with butter and seasonings.

USES: Winter radish makes an interesting salad ingredient but can also be cooked and served as a vegetable accompaniment, tasting rather like a turnip. It combines very well with coleslaw ingredients and with French beans in a salad.

RASPBERRIES

Raspberries, unlike some soft berry fruits, freeze exceptionally well. Consider growing your own, a visit to a pick-your-own fruit farm or buying in bulk at the market when at their peak since they can be used in countless dishes.

SELECTING FOR FREEZING

If you are picking your own fruit then do this on a dry day. Pick specimens that are just ripe and that do not show any signs of mouldiness, squashiness or uneven ripening. Check the same signs in shop-bought raspberries. Check the bottom of punnets, not just the best looking fruit on top, for signs of juice leaking or mould.

PREPARATION FOR FREEZING

Pick over the fruit and discard any that are not in prime condition. Hull and then grade into those that are perfect for freezing whole and those that are better made into a purée. Whole raspberries do not require any further preparation. Raspberries for a purée should be passed through a fine nylon sieve or puréed in a blender or food processor and then sieved to remove any pips. If you like, the purée can be sweetened with 100 g/4 oz sugar to every 450 g/1 lb prepared fruit. If you like, the raspberries can be lightly cooked with the absolute minimum of water and sugar prior to puréeing.

TO FREEZE

Whole raspberries can be frozen in a free-flow or dry sugar pack for success. For a free-flow pack, open freeze on trays until solid, then pack in polythene or rigid containers, seal, label and return to the freezer. For a dry sugar pack, pack in usable quantities in rigid containers, sprinkling each layer with sugar. Allow 100-175 g/4-6 oz sugar for every 450 g/1 lb fruit. Seal, label and freeze. Prepared raspberry purée should be poured in usable quantities into rigid containers, leaving a 2 cm/¾ inch headspace. Seal, label and freeze.

STORAGE TIME: Up to 12 months.

TO DEFROST AND SERVE: Whole raspberries should be left in their wrappings at room temperature for about 2 hours, when they will still be firm enough to add to fruit salads etc. Alternatively the raspberries can be cooked from frozen in hot pies and puddings. Thaw raspberry purée as for whole raspberries then use cold. Alternatively reheat from frozen over a very low heat to serve hot.

USES: In summer puddings, fruit puddings, pies, gâteaux, pastries, jam-making, to make raspberry vinegar, in mousses, fools, ice creams, sorbets and sauces.

RATATOUILLE

Everyone has a favourite ratatouille recipe and yours might contain anything or everything from courgettes, aubergines, onions and tomatoes to peppers, celery and herbs. As a made-up dish it freezes superbly and is an excellent way of using up the late summer glut of the vegetables and fruits above.

PREPARATION FOR FREEZING

Prepare your favourite recipe cooking until the mixture is just tender, adding seasonings, herbs and garlic as you like. Allow to cool completely.

TO FREEZE

Freeze in usable quantities in rigid containers, leaving a small headspace. Seal, label and freeze.

STORAGE TIME: Up to 6 months.

TO DEFROST AND SERVE: Cook from frozen over a very low heat without additional water until hot and tender. Alternatively, if intending to serve cold then defrost overnight in the refrigerator or for 4-6 hours at room temperature.

USES: Serve hot or cold as an accompanying vegetable, as a cold or hot starter sprinkled with grated Parmesan, or use as a filling for a tart or an omelette or hors d'oeuvres nibbles.

RED CABBAGE

See *Cabbage* (page 51)

RED MULLET

Red mullet is a delicious oily fish that has a rosy pink skin and delicate white flesh, usually weighing between 175-450 g/6-16 oz. The liver is considered a great delicacy, so leave inside the fish. It is in season between May and September.

SELECTING FOR FREEZING
Choose fish that is really fresh. Choose specimens with a firm flesh, clear, full and shiny eyes and a clean smell.

PREPARATION FOR FREEZING
Clean the fish but do not remove the liver. Rinse and pat dry with absorbent kitchen paper.

TO FREEZE
Wrap whole fish in cling film, then overwrap in polythene bags. Exclude as much air as possible and seal. Label and freeze.

STORAGE TIME: Up to 2 months.

TO DEFROST AND SERVE: Thaw whole fish in wrappings in the refrigerator overnight then cook as fresh.

USES: Red Mullet is best grilled or barbecued and is delicious if served with a maître d'Hôtel butter or a spicy salsa.

RICE

Since rice is very easy and quick to cook there often seems little point in preparing it especially for the freezer. However, if you have leftovers that may be wasted or you want to plan ahead for a party or want to make a rice mixture that can be reheated quickly to go with a main meal, there is ample justification.

PREPARATION FOR FREEZING
Cool any cooked rice completely before freezing. Mix with diced

vegetables and flavourings if liked to make a salad mixture or a pilaf-style dish and spoon into a rigid container. Seal, label and freeze.

STORAGE TIME: Plain boiled rice 4-6 months; made-up dishes up to 3 months (depending upon contents).

TO DEFROST AND SERVE: Reheat from frozen or thawed, in boiling salted water or in a covered container in a warm oven. Defrost cold rice mixtures for salads at room temperature for about 2 hours or overnight in the refrigerator.

USES: To make pilafs and risottos, rice salads, plain rice accompaniments to main meals and for adding to soups, hot-pots, casseroles and gratin-style dishes.

RHUBARB

Rhubarb freezes very successfully and can be stored in many different forms for year-round eating and enjoyment. Most of the rhubarb available in Britain comes from Cheshire and Yorkshire and is available as forced rhubarb from late winter through to early spring or as outdoor or natural rhubarb later in the year in May through to June.

SELECTING FOR FREEZING

Choose early or forced rhubarb that has the palest colour and the thinnest stems. Avoid any with bruised or blemished stems. Buying outdoor or natural rhubarb can be a bit of a lottery but in general avoid over large and over wieldy stems and reject those with over wieldy or limp leaves. Colour is not necessarily a good indicator since some varieties have a green and some a red stem and both freeze superbly.

PREPARATION FOR FREEZING

As soon as possible cut off the leaves and root ends, then wash the stems with cold running water. Rhubarb can be stored as cut pieces, stewed or as a purée. To prepare cut pieces, chop the prepared stems into short lengths about 5 cm/2 inches long. To prepare stewed rhubarb, cut as above then poach in the minimum amount of water with sugar to taste. The cooking time will not be very long so check frequently. Spices and flavourings can be added for extra flavour if you like. Allow to cool. To make a purée, poach as above then purée in a blender or food processor or pass through a fine nylon sieve. Add sugar to taste if you like and allow to cool.

TO FREEZE

Rhubarb pieces should ideally be blanched before freezing to preserve their colour. Blanch in boiling water for 1 minute, cool quickly in iced water then dry with absorbent kitchen paper. To make a free-flow pack, open freeze pieces on a tray until solid then pack into polythene bags or rigid containers, seal, label and return to the freezer. To make a dry sugar pack from rhubarb pieces, pack in usable quantities in rigid containers, sprinkling each layer with sugar. Allow 100 g/4 oz sugar to every 450 g/1 lb prepared fruit. Seal, label and freeze. Pack stewed rhubarb in usable quantities in rigid containers, leaving a 2 cm/¾ inch headspace. Seal, label and freeze.

STORAGE TIME: Up to 12 months.

TO DEFROST AND SERVE: Defrost free-flow and dry sugar packs at room temperature for 1-2 hours. Alternatively use from frozen in pies, puddings and crumbles, allowing a little extra cooking time. Thaw stewed rhubarb in its container at room temperature for about 3 hours. Thaw rhubarb purée in its container in the refrigerator overnight or at room temperature for about 3 hours.

USES: Use free-flow and dry sugar packs for pies, puddings and crumbles. Stewed rhubarb makes a wonderful dessert with cream or custard and can be used to make a pie filling. Use rhubarb purée to make fools, soufflés, mousses, sorbets and ice creams.

ROCK SALMON

Rock Salmon is a fish with firm, pinkish flesh that is usually sold already skinned. It is at its best from September through to April. It can be fried or cooked in the oven with butter and a light sprinkling of chopped mint. It is a popular fish to be fried in fish and chip shops.

For freezing follow the instructions for freezing BASS (see page 37).

RUNNER BEANS

Runner beans or stick beans are among the most popular vegetables frozen by the home gardener. They crop heavily and freeze well so are well worth the freezer space they take. Commercially grown beans are also available at a good price from July onwards and should be considered.

SELECTING FOR FREEZING

Choose young, fresh beans which snap cleanly if you try to break them open. The inner seeds should be small, plump and juicy. Avoid any that look old, tough and leathery.

PREPARATION FOR FREEZING

Top and tail as soon after picking or purchase. Wash thoroughly under cold running water. Remove any side strings. Very small beans can be frozen whole but the majority, it has to be said, should be sliced. Cut into slices about 2.5 cm/1 inch thick, either horizontally or diagonally.

TO FREEZE

Blanch any whole beans for 3 minutes in boiling water, drain, cool quickly in iced water, drain again and pat dry with absorbent kitchen paper. Open freeze on trays until solid. Pack in usable quantities in polythene bags. Seal, label and return to the freezer. Sliced beans should be blanched for 2 minutes in boiling water, drain, cool quickly in iced water, drain again and pat dry with absorbent kitchen paper. Open freeze on trays until solid. Pack in usable quantities in polythene bags. Seal, label and return to the freezer.

STORAGE TIME: Up to 12 months.

TO DEFROST AND SERVE: Cook whole frozen beans from frozen in boiling salted water for 7 minutes. Cook sliced beans in the same way but for 5 minutes.

USES: As a vegetable accompaniment boiled and tossed in butter with seasonings if you like. Use also in stir-fry and vegetable mixtures with a stir-fry sauce or herbs and garlic if you like.

SALADS

None of the usual salad ingredients like lettuce, watercress, tomatoes, onions and cucumber are any use for eating fresh and crisp after freezing. Their high moisture content makes them limp and watery after freezing.

SALMON

Salmon is a pink fleshed migratory fish which lives in the sea but comes up rivers to spawn. It is caught in the river, the season varying from early February to September, according to the river. Chilled or frozen Canadian and Pacific salmon can be bought outside the season of the home caught fish.

SELECTING FOR FREEZING

Look for fresh salmon (that hasn't previously been frozen) with firm, even-textured flesh, clear, full and shiny eyes, bright red gills and a clean smell.

PREPARATION FOR FREEZING

Freeze within 24 hours of the catch. Gut and clean, remove the scales and fins if you like but this is not necessary. Leave whole with the head and tail on if wished, or cut off the head and tail, split open and bone if you like. Rinse under cold running water and pat dry with absorbent kitchen paper. Whole salmon can also be cut into steaks or cutlets if preferred.

TO FREEZE

Wrap whole fish in cling film then overwrap in polythene. Exclude as much air as possible and seal, label and freeze. Interleave cutlets and steaks then pack together in polythene bags. Seal, label and freeze.

Sometimes a whole fresh salmon can be ice glazed for the freezer. This is a method of freezing that does not damage its skin as conventional freezer wraps might. It particularly suits salmon where the presentation of the skin can be all important. Gut and clean the fish, then open freeze on the fast-freeze control until solid. Dip in cold water, open freeze again, then repeat these two stages over and over again until a layer of ice about 5 mm/¼ inch thick has built up around the fish. Wrap tightly in cling film, polythene or foil, overwrap and seal before returning to the freezer.

STORAGE TIME: Up to 2 months.

TO DEFROST AND SERVE: Defrost whole fish in its wrappings in the refrigerator overnight if large then cook as for fresh. Smaller whole fish can be defrosted in the refrigerator for 1 hour, then cooked as for fresh, allowing a little extra time. Defrost cutlets and steaks in the same way and cook as for fresh, allowing a little extra time. Defrost ice-glazed whole fish in the refrigerator overnight until completely thawed.

USES: Whole salmon are usually poached or baked and served with sauces. Cutlets and steaks are usually grilled, poached or baked. When served hot, the fish steaks and cutlets and the whole fish can be accompanied with a Hollandaise, butter or cucumber sauce and when cold, with mayonnaise or a tartare sauce. Salmon is also delicious flaked into rice mixtures, pasta dishes, salads and sandwich fillings.

SALMON TROUT

This is a fish similar in shape and habitat to the salmon but narrower and smaller. The flesh is less firm and more delicate and is generally cooked whole. It is at its best during the summer months from March to July. It is particularly good poached and served cold. Because it is less expensive than salmon it is quite often sold and served as a salmon substitute.

For freezing follow the instructions for freezing TROUT (see page 163).

SALSIFY

Salsify is a white vegetable with a long, tapering root. A similar plant of the same family is known as scorzonera, but this is black on the outside. It is suitable for freezing and serving as a vegetable accompaniment.

SELECTING FOR FREEZING
Select young, tender roots. Usually at their peak from October to November.

PREPARATION FOR FREEZING
Scrub well but do not peel before blanching.

TO FREEZE
Blanch for 2 minutes in boiling water. Drain, cut into 5 cm/2 inch strips and peel while still warm. Cool in iced water, drain again and pat dry with absorbent kitchen paper. Pack, in usable quantities in polythene bags. Seal, label and freeze.

STORAGE TIME: 12 months.

TO DEFROST AND SERVE: Cook in boiling salted water until tender, about 5-8 minutes.

USES: As a vegetable accompaniment tossed in butter and seasonings or coated with a béchamel sauce. Alternatively, leave to cool and toss in a lemony dressing and serve as a salad dish.

SANDWICHES

White and brown bread sandwiches freeze well. All varieties can be frozen – closed, rolled, club, pinwheel, open or ribbon. Do not freeze sandwiches containing hard-boiled egg, salad, mayonnaise and sliced fresh tomato since these fillings do not freeze well. Pack as individual sandwiches or in stacks of the same filling, interleaved with foil. Wrap in heavy-duty foil or in a polythene bag. Seal, label and freeze.

STORAGE TIME: Open sandwiches 1 week; all others up to 2 months.

TO DEFROST AND SERVE: Leave in the packaging. All sandwiches can be left overnight in the refrigerator or defrosted at room temperature. Times vary depending upon size of the package. Individually wrapped take 2 hours; stacks of 4-6 sandwiches 6-7 hours; rolled sandwiches 4-5 hours.

Pinwheel, club and ribbon sandwiches, which cut more easily when partially defrosted, take 3-4 hours; open sandwiches take 1-2 hours. Garnish with salad after defrosting if you like.

See also *Toasted Sandwiches* (page 161).

SATSUMAS

The satsuma is similar to the tangerine in both taste and appearance but to the would-be freezer cook it has one outstanding advantage – it contains no pips! Since it has a relatively short season, around Christmas time, it is well worth freezing a quantity for year-round enjoyment.

SELECTING FOR FREEZING

Buy shiny, firm fruit with smooth and plump, never dry or shrivelled-looking skins. Choose specimens that weigh heavy for their size – it is a reliable sign that the fruit are juicy.

PREPARATION FOR FREEZING

Peel, then separate into segments, removing any excess pith.

TO FREEZE

Pack in usable quantities in rigid containers, sprinkling between each layer with sugar to taste. Alternatively, cover the segments with a medium sugar syrup (see page 25). Seal, label and freeze.

STORAGE TIME: Freeze for up to 12 months.

TO DEFROST AND SERVE: Defrost frozen satsuma segments in their container for about 2 hours at room temperature.

USES: In fruit salads, breakfast citrus dishes or fruit-based desserts.

SAUCES

Almost all sauces freeze well and are tremendous time savers to have in the freezer. Make double quantities when preparing the sauce to eat fresh and freeze the other half, or make a large quantity when convenient.

PREPARATION FOR FREEZING

Any good cookery book will give the details and recipes and cooking instructions for individual sauces. Some people prefer to use cornflour rather than plain flour in making a sauce for the freezer, as it helps to minimise any separation on defrosting and reheating.

TO FREEZE

If packing in rigid containers then remember to leave a 2 cm/¾ inch headspace for expansion. Pack in quantities suitable to your needs, 150,300, 450 or 600 ml/¼,½,¾, or 1 pint quantities perhaps, or in cubes from an ice cube tray. One ice cube usually equals about 15 ml/1 tablespoon and small quantities, like 30-45 ml/2-3 tablespoons are often useful in coating or binding food. This is also a good reason and way for freezing small quantities of leftover sauce which might otherwise be wasted. Sauces that can be frozen this way include:

BASIC WHITE ROUX (the basis also for cheese, parsley, rum or brandy sauce etc)

BÉCHAMEL SAUCE (the basis for Mornay, prawn, onion and vanilla sauce etc)

VELOUTÉ SAUCE (the basis for a creamy curry, dill, anchovy, mustard and white wine sauce etc)

ESPAGNOLE OR BASIC BROWN SAUCE (the basis for a curry or red wine sauce etc)

And also: Bolognese Sauce, Sweet and Sour Sauce, Barbecue Sauce, Tomato Sauce Mushroom Sauce, Orange Sauce, Chocolate Sauce, Fruit Purée Sauce and Butterscotch Sauce.

STORAGE TIME: About 3-4 months, depending upon ingredients. The spicier the sauce the shorter the storage time.

TO DEFROST AND SERVE: Either defrost in the refrigerator and reheat, or gently reheat from frozen, preferably in a double saucepan or in a bowl over a pan of boiling water to avoid any sticking. Any separation or lumpiness can usually be beaten out with a whisk. Cream or eggs added to enrich the sauce are best added just before serving.

SAUCES NOT SUITABLE FOR FREEZING INCLUDE:

Mayonnaise, Tartare, Rémoulade, Hollandaise and Bérnaise.

SAUSAGES

It is doubtful if it is worth making your own sausages for the freezer but it is definitely worth finding a good butcher who specialises in making his own and whose recipe you like. Buy them fresh and check that they have not been previously frozen.

PREPARATION AND TO FREEZE

Pack, in usable quantities, using interleave to separate the links. Wrap in foil or in polythene bags. Seal, label and freeze.

STORAGE TIME: About 2 months if not too spicy; if spicy then up to 4 weeks.

TO DEFROST AND SERVE: Defrost completely before cooking. Defrost slowly in the refrigerator overnight for best results, or 3-4 hours at room temperature.

SAUSAGEMEAT

Pack in usable quantities for making meatballs, stuffings and other made-up dishes.

To freeze follow the instructions for freezing SAUSAGES (see above).

SCALLOPS

A scallop is a shell fish in two ribbed shells with undulating edges. It is usually sold opened and attached to the deep shell (the shells make ideal cooking utensils). Scallops are often poached in milk or a flavourome fish stock and served in a sauce. They are at their best in January, February and March.

For freezing follow the freezing instructions for freezing MUSSELS (page 114).

SCAMPI

Dublin Bay prawns or Pacific prawns are classed as scampi. They can be bought fresh or cooked and are ideal for freezing. Check that they haven't been frozen previously. They are in season all year round but are at their best from February to October. Scampi are often breaded and deep fried but can also be cooked in a tomato and onion mixture. Frozen tails should be cooked for 4-6 minutes in boiling salted water, drained and cooled before freezing if cooked scampi are required.

For freezing follow the instructions for freezing PRAWNS (see page 135).

SCONES

As fresh scones take very little time to prepare and bake there is little point in freezing them uncooked. They do however freeze well when already baked and are useful tea-time standbys in the freezer.

PREPARATION
Prepare as usual using a recipe for plain, fruited or cheese scones.

TO FREEZE
Wrap cooled scones in foil or polythene bags. Seal, label and freeze.

STORAGE TIME: Plain and fruited up to 6 months; cheese scones up to 3 months.

TO DEFROST AND SERVE: Leave in the packaging at room temperature for 1-1½ hours or, preferably place frozen, wrapped in foil, in a moderately hot oven, 200°C/400°F/Gas 6, for 10 minutes. Serve while still warm.

SCORZONERA

For freezing follow the instructions for freezing SALSIFY (page 146).

SHORTBREAD

See *Biscuits* (page 41).

SHRIMPS

For freezing follow the instructions for freezing PRAWNS (see page 135).

SKATE

Skate is a large fish of which only the wings are used for food. It can be fried and poached and is generally served with black butter. The fishmonger usually removes the dark skin before offering the fish for sale. Skate is caught mainly off the Cornish coasts of England and here the liver is used. It can be poached and served with the fish or after poaching, it can be marinated in oil and lemon juice, then coated with batter and deep fried. Skate is available from October to April.

For freezing follow the instructions for freezing COD (see page 69).

SMOKED HADDOCK

Smoked haddock is sold either in fillets or split and smoked whole. The latter are called Finnan Haddie and the best comes from Aberdeen. This is haddock traditionally smoked over peat smoke.

SELECTING AND PREPARING FOR FREEZING

Only freeze freshly smoked fish, not fish that has been previously frozen and thawed. Leave whole with tails on if wished or cut off. Remove the skin from whole fish or fillets if you like.

TO FREEZE

Wrap individual whole fish in cling film then overwrap in polythene bags. Exclude as much air as possible and seal, label and freeze.

Interleave fillets then pack together in bags, seal, label and freeze.

STORAGE TIME: Up to 3 months.

TO DEFROST AND SERVE: Thaw in the wrappings in the refrigerator for about 1 hour, then cook as fresh smoked fish, allowing extra time.

USES: Serve cooked smoked haddock plain with butter and seasonings, or with an egg sauce. It can also be used to make an omelette filling and flaked into rice to make the classic English breakfast dish, Kedgeree.

SNIPE

This is a small game bird similar to woodcock. When preparing snipe, the head is left on and apart from removing the gizzard it is not drawn. When trussing, the long beak is used to hold it in shape. Snipe are in season from August to January but considered at their best in November. It is best barded and roasted for about 10 minutes after defrosting. It can however be grilled or roasted on the spit. Allow one bird per person when serving.

For freezing follow the instructions for freezing WOODCOCK (see page 171) but remember not to draw the bird, simply remove the gizzard.

SOLE

Sole is a flat fish with firm, white flesh and a delicate flavour. There are four main kinds: Dover Sole, Lemon Sole, Torbay Sole or megrim and Witch Sole, the first two being the main ones eaten in Britain. The Dover

Sole is more elongated in shape than the others and can be distinguised by its dark, greyish-black skin on the upper side. It is generally considered the most superior in flavour. Dover Sole is available from June to January and Lemon Sole from December to March.

For freezing follow the instructions for freezing COD (see page 69).

SORBETS

As sorbets obviously contain a lot of water, the home-made variety forms larger crystals than commercially made, which is frozen much quicker at a lower temperature.

The sorbet mixture should be put into the freezer until mushy then the whisked egg whites should be folded in gently. This method reduces the amount of large ice crystals that will be formed.

STORAGE TIME: Up to 3 months.

TO DEFROST AND SERVE: Before serving, place in the refrigerator for 10-15 minutes to soften slightly. This will help with scooping.

SOUFFLÉS

Cooked varieties of soufflé can only be frozen before baking and taken up to the stage of adding the stiffly beaten egg whites. Cold, sweet and savoury soufflés freeze exceptionally well. Use foil collars rather than greaseproof ones and secure firmly with freezer tape. Pour in the prepared mixture, but do not decorate until the time of serving. Open freeze until solid then transfer to a polythene bag or rigid container. Seal, label and return to the freezer.

STORAGE TIME: 3 months.

TO DEFROST AND SERVE: For cold soufflés, remove the collar carefully as soon as it is taken from the freezer. Defrost in the refrigerator overnight, or leave at room temperature for about 4 hours. When defrosted, decorate as you like and serve chilled.

Leave mixtures for baking to defrost at room temperature until thawed, about 4-5 hours. Add the egg whites and bake in the normal way.

SOUPS

All kinds of soups respond well to storage in the freezer. The following notes are useful to know.

Concentrated soup takes up less room in the freezer but remember to dilute accordingly.

Freeze in quantities likely for family use or freeze in ice cube trays so that as many or as few may be removed as required.

If cream is to be added, do so on reheating so that the storage time is not reduced to that of the cream.

Leave a 2 cm/¾ inch headspace when freezing to allow for expansion. Pack in rigid containers, seal, label and freeze.

STORAGE TIME: 3-6 months, depending upon ingredients.

SPINACH

There are two different kinds of spinach – the winter or prickly-seeded spinach and the summer or round-seeded spinach. Both can be frozen successfully.

SELECTING FOR FREEZING

The best time for freezing spinach is in March and April. Choose young leaves. Avoid any spinach which has yellow, limp or damaged leaves. Be suspicious of large fibrous stalks or flower heads, this is an indication of over-maturity.

PREPARATION FOR FREEZING

Snap off the stalks, then wash each leaf individually under cold running water to remove all signs of dirt or grit. Leaves can be left whole or can be torn into smaller pieces.

TO FREEZE

Blanch the leaves in boiling water for 2 minutes. Drain well, pressing the leaves with the back of a wooden spoon to extract as much moisture as possible. Cool and then place in usable quantities in polythene bags. Seal, label and freeze.

STORAGE TIME: Up to 12 months.

TO DEFROST AND SERVE: Cook spinach from frozen in a heavy-based pan, without any additional water, for about 5 minutes. Add a little melted butter and seasonings. Ground nutmeg and mace are good seasonings. Serve as leaves or purée in a blender or food processor to make a spinach purée if you like.

153

USES: Serve as a vegetable accompaniment topped with grated Parmesan if you like, or use in soups, quiches, pastries and made-up pasta dishes like lasagne.

SPRATS

Sprats are small silvery fish of the herring family. They are rich and oily and can be barbecued, baked or grilled. Sprats are at their best in the winter from November to February. They are very good sprinkled with flour and baked.

For freezing follow the instructions for freezing TROUT (see page 163).

SQUAB

A squab is a young pigeon especially bred for the table. It is normally about 4 weeks old and weighs between 350-675 g/12-24 oz. Squab is prepared and drawn in the same way as other domesticated birds. It is available in May and June. It is a very tender bird and can be roasted, sautéed, grilled or stewed.

For freezing follow the instructions for freezing WOODCOCK (page 171) but remember to draw the bird before roasting.

STEAMED SPONGE PUDDING

Puddings made from plain or rich cake mixtures and quick mixes can be frozen equally well before or after freezing. Basins made of foil or polythene are the most suitable, but if only glass or earthernware dishes are available then line with greased foil and remove the puddings from the basins when frozen and seal in the usual way.

PREPARATION FOR FREEZING
Make puddings in the usual way adding flavourings and toppings.

TO FREEZE
Uncooked puddings: seal basins tightly with heavy-duty foil, label and freeze immediately.
Cooked puddings: cool completely and seal basins with heavy-duty foil. Label and freeze at once.

STORAGE TIME: Uncooked puddings and cooked puddings up to 3 months.

TO DEFROST AND SERVE: Remove the packaging, cover with greased foil and place the frozen pudding in a steamer.
Uncooked puddings – a 1 kg/2 lbs pudding should be steamed for 2½ hours to defrost and cook.
Cooked puddings – a 1 kg/2 lbs pudding should be steamed for 45 minutes to defrost and heat through.

STEWS

For freezing follow the instructions for freezing CASSEROLES (page 57)

STOCK

Stock is a very useful product to have in the freezer, especially in concentrated form – remember to dilute to taste.

PREPARATION AND TO FREEZE

Prepare as usual and allow to cool. When cold, pour into rigid containers, leaving a 2 cm/¾ inch headspace. Seal, label and freeze.

STORAGE TIME: 2-3 months for basic stocks; up to 2 weeks for highly seasoned stocks.

TO DEFROST AND USE: Either defrost for 1-2 hours at room temperature, or heat immediately until boiling point is reached.

USES: In soups, sauces, casseroles, stews and any made-up dish requiring a good stock in the ingredients.

STRAWBERRIES

Although almost everyone's favourite fruit, strawberries are not as successful in the freezer as one might hope. The result is a rather squashy, watery fruit if care is not taken in selecting the best variety and following the recommended defrosting procedure.

SELECTING FOR FREEZING

Choose just ripe, unblemished fruit. If you are growing your own then consider the following varieties for better than average freezing results: Cambridge Favourites, Cambridge Rival, Cambridge Vigour, Gento and Grandee.

PREPARATION FOR FREEZING

Remove the hulls and wash or wipe only if necessary. Slice, mash or purée if preferred.

TO FREEZE

Open freeze whole strawberries on trays until solid then pack, in usable quantities, in polythene bags. Seal, label and return to the freezer.

Alternatively, layer with sugar in a rigid container, using 100 g/4 oz sugar to every 450 g/1 lb fruit. Seal, label and freeze.

Another option is to pack the strawberries, in usable quantities, in rigid boxes and to cover them with a heavy sugar syrup (see page 25). Leave a 2 cm/¾ inch headspace. Seal, label and freeze.

STORAGE TIME: 12 months.

TO DEFROST AND SERVE: Single whole strawberries can take from 20-30 minutes to defrost at room temperature; 35-45 minutes in the refrigerator. It is best to eat them with a few ice crystals remaining. For a 450 g/1 lb pack, defrost for 4-5 hours in the refrigerator; 2-3 hours at room temperature.

Defrost sugar and syrup pack strawberries in their unopened containers for 2-3 hours at room temperature, turning the pack during defrosting.

USES: Frozen strawberries are best used in desserts where their appearance is not of paramount importance - in pies, glazed flans, creams, mousses and trifles for example. Even after preparing as above some people still find the quality unacceptable. If this is the case then it is better to freeze the strawberries as a purée for later use in soufflés, mousses etc.

STUFFINGS

Stuffings may be completely prepared and then frozen. The storage life will be that of the lowest life ingredient. Remember seasonings will intensify. Do not stuff meat, fish or poultry as it will reduce that item's storage life to that of the stuffing. Pack in quantities likely for use. Pack into polythene bags, seal, label and freeze. Breadcrumbs in the freezer mean all kinds of stuffing can easily be made from fresh.

SUET

Suet can be shredded and frozen. Pack in known quantities suitable for recipe use. STORAGE TIME: 5 months.

SUET PUDDINGS

To freeze follow the instructions for freezing STEAMED SPONGE PUDDINGS (see page 154).

SWEDE

The swede is a coarse root vegetable rather like a large turnip but yellow in colour. It freezes well.

SELECTING FOR FREEZING
Choose small, young swedes.

PREPARATION FOR FREEZING
Remove the tops, wash, peel and dice.

TO FREEZE
Blanch in boiling water for 2 minutes, although this is not necessary for short storage or if used as part of a stew pack. Alternatively, cook completely and purée for freezing.

Pack blanched swede in usable quantities in polythene bags. Seal, label and freeze.

Allow purée to cool then pack, in usable quantities, in rigid containers, leaving a 2 cm/¾ inch headspace. Seal, label and freeze.

STORAGE TIME: 9-12 months for blanched swede; 8-10 months for purée; up to 3 months for unblanched and stew pack swede.

TO DEFROST AND SERVE: Cook from frozen except for the purée. Allow the purée to defrost unopened until soft, about 2-3 hours at room temperature.

Cook in boiling water for 8-12 minutes or reheat the purée over a gentle heat.

USES: In stews, soups and casseroles. Purées are good in soups and for mixing with baby food.

SWEETCORN

Sweetcorn is probably best frozen as corn on the cob. It really isn't worth the effort to remove the kernels from the cob to freeze (and commercially prepared sweetcorn is so good anyway). If you really do want to freeze your own kernels then the method is outlined below.

SELECTING FOR FREEZING

Select cobs that are uniformly matured. Select produce where the kernels are well rounded and the milk is thin and sweet, not starchy.

PREPARATION FOR FREEZING

Remove the husks and silks and wash well. Grade cobs to be frozen whole according to size.

To prepare kernels, hold the corn stem upwards and with a sharp knife cut down as near to the cob as possible. Continue around the cob until all the corn kernels have been removed.

TO FREEZE

Blanch similar-sized cobs together; small cobs in boiling water for 4 minutes; medium cobs for 5 minutes; and large cobs for 6 minutes. Drain, cool in iced water, drain again, pat dry with absorbent kitchen paper then pack singly or in pairs in polythene bags. Seal, label and freeze.

Corn kernels should be blanched for 2 minutes. Drain, cool in iced water, drain again and pat dry with absorbent kitchen paper. Pack, in usable quantities, in polythene bags. Seal, label and freeze.

STORAGE TIME: 12 months.

TO DEFROST AND SERVE: Corn on the cobs should be completely defrosted before cooking, otherwise the kernels become cooked with the cob possibly still frozen. Defrosting takes about 3-4 hours at room temperature.

Kernels can be cooked from frozen. Cook in boiling water for 5-8 minutes.

USES: Serve whole cobs as starters or with barbecue fare. Kernels make a good vegetable accompaniment and are good to use in stir-fries, rice mixtures and made-up dishes that appreciate their sweet taste and good colour.

SWISS CHARD

Also known as seakale beet or spinach beet, this is a type of beet which is grown for its edible leaves rather than its root. It is in fact two vegetables in one, since the glossy green leaves can be eaten like spinach and the white midrib stalks make a tasty vegetable in their own right.

SELECTING FOR FREEZING

Swiss Chard is usually available from early spring right through to early autumn depending upon when the seeds are sown. Pick or buy when young and fresh looking before the leaves have grown too large and the stalks are not tough.

PREPARATION FOR FREEZING

Wash each leaf individually under cold running water to remove all dirt then strip the leaves away from the central stalk. Trim the stalks at each end, then cut into 5 cm/2 inch lengths, dividing them lengthways if they are very thick.

TO FREEZE

Blanch the leaves in boiling water for 2 minutes, drain and cool in iced water. Drain again and pat dry with absorbent kitchen paper and squeeze dry. Pack in usable quantities in polythene bags. Seal, label and freeze. Blanch the stalks for 3 minutes in boiling water, drain and cool in iced water. Drain again and pat dry with absorbent kitchen paper. Pack in usable quantities in polythene bags. Seal, label and freeze. Alternatively mix at this stage with a béchamel or cheese sauce and pack for the freezer.

STORAGE TIME: Up to 12 months.

TO DEFROST AND SERVE: Cook leaves from frozen in a saucepan with melted butter and seasonings. Cook for about 5 minutes. Cook frozen sliced stalks in boiling salted water for about 7 minutes.

USES: The leaves can be served as a vegetable accompaniment or in any recipe as a substitute for spinach (perfect for soups and quiches). The stalks can also be served as a vegetable accompaniment like celery and can be cooked in a sauce like cheese or béchamel. Sprinkled with breadcrumbs and Parmesan they also make a fine gratin dish.

SWISS ROLLS

See *Cakes* (page 53)

TANGERINES

Tangerines, like satsumas, mandarins and clementines, have a short season so are worth freezing for year-round enjoyment. They are however the variety with the most number of pips so preparation can be a little more lengthy if you insist upon depipping before freezing.

SELECTING FOR FREEZING

Buy shiny, firm fruit with plump, never dry or shrivelled-looking skins. Choose specimens that weigh heavy for their size - it is a sure sign that they are juicy.

PREPARATION FOR FREEZING

Peel, then separate into segments, removing excess pith and pips if you wish.

TO FREEZE

Pack in usable quantities in rigid containers, sprinkling between each layer with sugar to taste. Alternatively, cover the segments with a medium sugar syrup (see page 25). Seal, label and freeze.

STORAGE TIME: Freeze for up to 12 months.

TO DEFROST AND SERVE: Defrost frozen tangerine segments in their container for about 2 hours at room temperature.

USES: In fruit salads, breakfast citrus dishes or fruit-based desserts.

TARTS

For freezing follow the instructions for freezing QUICHES and PASTRY (pages 137 and 122).

TEABREADS

Baked in the usual way and then frozen, teabreads can prove a useful and delicious treat for tea-time eating.

PREPARATION FOR FREEZING: Bake in the usual way and cool quickly.

TO FREEZE

Freeze in polythene bags in convenient slices for serving. Seal, label and freeze.

STORAGE TIME: 6 months.

❄

TO DEFROST AND SERVE: Defrost teabreads in their wrapping at
room temperature for 2-3 hours.

TOASTED SANDWICHES

Sandwiches for toasting can also be stored in the freezer. Prepare suitable
fillings, avoiding hard-boiled egg, mayonnaise, salad and tomato. Prepare,
pack and store as for SANDWICHES (page 146). Unwrap and place
frozen under the grill to defrost and cook, they defrost while toasting.
Use a slightly lower temperature for toasting and a few minutes extra
cooking time to normal.

TOMATOES

The ordinary round tomato is the most common type cultivated for
eating and is probably the most favoured for freezing. Consider freezing
whole, as a purée, juice or sauce when prices are especially low or you
have a bumper home-grown crop. Also consider freezing big beefsteak,
tiny cherry and intensely-flavoured plum tomatoes when there is a glut
and their fine flavours can be appreciated in cooked dishes.

SELECTING FOR FREEZING
Choose firm, just ripe, medium-sized ordinary round tomatoes or cherry,
plum or beefsteak tomatoes in peak condition for freezing whole. They
can't be used for salads but can be added to countless cooked dishes
where their colour and flavour are invaluable and will also fry and grill
with success. Ideally choose under rather than over-ripe specimens when
in season from June to October. However, tomatoes that are to be frozen
as a juice or a purée can be very ripe and on the soft side. Look out for
super low-priced bargains and if in doubt about the quality, taste before
buying in quantity, to check the flavour. Green and under-ripe tomatoes
are best used to make chutney, rather than frozen.

PREPARATION FOR FREEZING
WHOLE TOMATOES: Remove the stalks and wipe with a damp cloth.
There is no need to skin. Especially large beefsteak tomatoes can be
halved or quartered if you wish.

TOMATOES FOR JUICE: Skin the tomatoes if you wish then chop
coarsely and purée in a food processor or blender until smooth. Transfer
to a pan and cook over a low heat for about 5-10 minutes. Strain through
a sieve to remove any pips or skin and allow to cool completely.

TOMATOES FOR PURÉE: Prepare as for juice but cook, uncovered, until a thick purée is formed, about 30 minutes, then allow to cool completely.

TOMATOES FOR A SAUCE: Skin and deseed tomatoes, chop coarsely and place in a pan with onions, garlic, herbs and other seasonings to taste. Simmer gently for about 1 hour then blend to a purée. Allow to cool completely.

TO FREEZE

WHOLE TOMATOES: Pack in usable quantities in plastic freezer bags. Seal, label and freeze.

HALVED AND QUARTERED TOMATOES: Pack in a single layer in rigid containers. Seal, label and freeze.

TOMATO JUICE, TOMATO PURÉE AND TOMATO SAUCE: Pour usable quantities into rigid containers, leaving a 2 cm/¾ inch headspace. Seal, label and freeze.

STORAGE TIME: Freeze for up to 12 months.

TO DEFROST AND SERVE

WHOLE TOMATOES: Defrost in their plastic freezer bags at room temperature for about 2 hours. Use in cooking the same way as you would use fresh tomatoes.

TOMATO HALVES AND QUARTERS: Grill or fry from frozen allowing 1-2 minutes extra cooking time.

TOMATO JUICE: Defrost in its container in the refrigerator until liquid, about 2-4 hours.

TOMATO PURÉE AND TOMATO SAUCE: Defrost as for juice or heat in a thick-based saucepan very gently to defrost and reheat for use in dishes, stirring frequently.

USES: Whole, halved and quartered tomatoes can be grilled or fried for use as meal accompaniments. Tomato juice can be served as a drink or used in soups, sauces and casseroles. Tomato purée and sauce can be used in soups, sauces, hot-pots, casseroles and countless pasta dishes. Tomato sauce is a home-made must for hamburgers, grills, meat-loaves and barbecue fare - much nicer than commercial offerings!

TROUT

Trout is a fresh-water fish found in rivers, lakes and streams. The flesh is very delicate and varies in colour from white to pink according to the waters it inhabits. Trout comes in many varieties: brook, lake, steelhead, brown and salmon but perhaps the most popular is the rainbow trout.

SELECTING FOR FREEZING
When buying trout and other oily fish look for fresh fish with firm, even-textured flesh, clear, full and shiny eyes, bright red gills and a clean smell.

PREPARATION FOR FREEZING
Freeze within 24 hours of the catch. Gut and clean, remove the scales and fins. Leave whole with the heads and tails on if wished, or cut off heads and tails, split open and bone. Rinse under cold running water and pat dry with absorbent kitchen paper.

TO FREEZE
Wrap individual whole fish in cling film then overwrap in polythene bags. Exclude as much air as possible and seal, label and freeze.
    Interleave fillets then pack together in bags, seal, label and freeze.

STORAGE TIME: Up to 2 months.

TO DEFROST AND SERVE: Defrost whole fish in its wrappings in the refrigerator for about 1 hour, then cook as fresh allowing extra time. Cook boned fish and fillets from frozen, allowing extra time.

USES: Trout can be baked, poached, sautéed, barbecued and grilled.

TURBOT

This is a highly prized fish, known as the king of flat fish. The flesh is firm and white and somewhat gelatinous. It can weigh as much as 9-13.5 kg/20-30 lbs. The smaller fish, 3-4 kg/6-8 lbs are known as chicken turbot. Turbot can be boiled, steamed or baked.

For freezing follow the instructions for freezing COD (see page 69).

TURKEYS

Whilst it is possible to buy a fresh turkey at almost any time of the year these days, it is far easier, the choices are greater and the prices are keener around the Christmas and Easter festivities. Many supermarkets in particular will often price their turkeys very competitively as a 'loss leader' in the hope of getting Christmas food shoppers through their doors. This may well then be the best time to consider freezing an extra turkey or two to enjoy when fresh supplies are scarce during the summer months.

RAW TURKEYS
SELECTING FOR FREEZING

Choose young plump birds. The recommended size for home freezing is 5-8 kg/8-15 lbs. It should be borne in mind that the larger the turkey, the higher flesh-to-bone ratio, therefore bigger birds are often better value for money. On the negative side remember just how much space a very large turkey will take in your freezer. Select fleshy birds with a light layering of fat under the skin, with the skin untorn and not blemished in any way.

PREPARATION FOR FREEZING

Pluck and hang if necessary. Singe small remaining feathers and hairs over a flame. Remove head and feet, and draw the entrails, separating the giblets (which should be frozen separately from the poultry if a long storage life is desired). If several turkeys are being prepared for freezing then it is worth separating the livers for use in recipes on their own. Chill thoroughly in the refrigerator.

TO FREEZE

Whole birds should be prepared as for cooking with legs and wings well trussed to the body to give a compact shape. Place a small pad of foil over any protruding bones so that they do not puncture the packaging. Wrap in a gusseted polythene bag taking care to mould around the turkey removing as much air as possible. Seal, label and freeze.

NB It is not advisable to stuff turkey before freezing because the stuffing itself takes a long time to reach the desired low temperature, thus giving possible food spoilage organisms the time and warm conditions necessary for their growth. The storage time in the freezer would be reduced to that of the stuffing (little over a month) making unstuffed poultry a much more desirable freezer product.
Pack giblets in a rigid container. Seal, label and freeze.

STORAGE TIME: 8-10 months for whole turkey; 3 months for giblets.

TO DEFROST AND SERVE: ALL TURKEYS MUST BE COMPLETELY DEFROSTED BEFORE COOKING. Defrost at room temperature for the times below (alternatively defrost in the refrigerator but the times will be 2-3 times as long):

WEIGHT	AT ROOM TEMP
2.7 kg/6 lb	14 hours
4 kg/9 lb	36 hours
6 kg/14 lb	48 hours
9 kg/20 lb	60 hours

Giblets should be defrosted in their container in the refrigerator for about 12 hours.

USES: Turkeys make a wonderful low-fat main meal option and can be roasted and served with accompaniments like stuffing, bread sauce, cranberry sauce, bacon rolls,chipolata sausages and a thin gravy. Giblets can be used to make stock, pâtés and can be lightly sautéed to serve with pasta or rice.

TURKEY PORTIONS

Turkey portions should be prepared like whole birds, but cut into portions suitable to your family's requirements. Trim into neat portions of legs, breasts and wings or chopped turkey meat. Either pack separately, or pack together separating each portion with interleaving paper for easy removal when required. Thaw completely before cooking as above.

STORAGE TIME: 8-10 months.

USES: Portions can be roasted, grilled, sautéed, barbecued, casseroled, fried and used to make soups and other made-up dishes.

COOKED TURKET MEAT

Whole turkeys and portions may be cooked and frozen on or off the bone and are useful for advance preparation for parties and picnic meals. Slices of turkey can also be frozen and are best when covered with gravy which prevents any drying out. **NB** Turkey that has been frozen once in its cooked state should never be defrosted and then refrozen.

STORAGE TIMES: Cooked whole bird up to 2 months; casseroled or in gravy up to 2 months; and slices of turkey not in a sauce or gravy up to 1 month.

TURNIPS

Turnips do appear on the market as early as spring but the main crop, which is the best to freeze, does not arrive until the autumn. They can be frozen alone or as part of a stew pack.

SELECTING FOR FREEZING

Choose small to medium-sized turnips that have firm and undamaged roots. If the specimens have bright green leaves that are not wilted they are a sure sign of freshness.

PREPARATION FOR FREEZING

Wash, then top and tail. Peel thinly and leave whole if small or cut larger ones into 1-2 cm/½-¾ inch dice. Alternatively make a purée by cooking diced turnips in boiling salted water for about 10 minutes until tender. Drain and then mash or purée in a food processor or blender. Cool completely before freezing.

TO FREEZE

Whole and diced turnips should be blanched before freezing in boiling water for 2-3 minutes. Drain and cool in iced water, drain again and pat dry with absorbent kitchen paper. Open freeze until solid, pack in usable quantities in polythene bags. Seal, label and return to the freezer. Turnip purée should be packed in usable quantities in rigid containers, leaving a 2 cm/¾ inch headspace. Seal, label and freeze.

STORAGE TIME: Up to 12 months.

TO DEFROST AND SERVE: Cook whole and diced turnips from frozen in boiling salted water for 5-10 minutes, depending upon size. Or add from frozen to soups, stews and casseroles. Reheat turnip purée from frozen in a double boiler.

USES: Whole and diced turnips can be used as a vegetable accompaniment, in stews, casseroles and soups. Turnip purée can also be served as a vegetable accompaniment with butter and seasonings. It can also be added to mashed potato to make a topping for pies.

UGLI FRUIT

This fruit is a cross between a grapefruit and a tangerine. It has a loose, wrinkled skin that is tinged with green. Underneath its very ugli skin is a juicy sweet flesh all the better for sampling!

SELECTION FOR FREEZING

Ugli fruit are generally available only throughout the winter months.

They are worth freezing to enjoy during the summer months.

PREPARATION FOR FREEZING
Peel, then separate into segments, removing all pith.

TO FREEZE
Open freeze segments on a plastic tray until solid, then pack into polythene bags. Seal, label and return to the freezer. Alternatively, pack segments in usable quantities in rigid containers, either sprinkling between each layer with sugar to taste or covering the fruit segments with a light sugar syrup (see page 25). Leave a small headspace if the latter method is used. Seal, label and freeze.

STORAGE TIME: Up to 12 months.

TO DEFROST AND SERVE: Leave to stand in the wrappings or container at room temperature for about 2 hours, then use as for fresh ugli fruit.

USES: In fruit salads, breakfast citrus mixtures and in any recipe as a substitute for oranges.

VEAL

It is doubtful (as it is rarely inexpensive) that you would want to freeze a large quantity of veal. However, occasionally your butcher or freezer centre may have a few selected cuts on special offer which you may want to give freezer space to. For example, you may consider buying a boned and rolled shoulder to roast, one or two packs of diced stewing veal for fricassés and pies and a pack of escalopes for quick frying.

SELECTING FOR FREEZING
Follow the guidelines for BEEF (page 38) although the flesh is likely to be paler in colour. Joints will come from the leg (the cushion, silverside and thick flank); the loin (sold on the bone and boned and rolled); best end (ribs); breast (boned and rolled); shoulder (boned and rolled); neck (including middle neck and best end of neck); and the flank (rolled).

Chops, cutlets, escalopes and medallions will come from the following areas: the fillet end of leg will be cut into escalopes and medallions; the loin will be divided into chops; the loin fillet sliced in medallions; and the best end ribs and middle neck will be divided into cutlets.

Minced veal will come from the shoulder and flank.

PREPARATION FOR FREEZING AND TO FREEZE

JOINTS (for roasting/slow roasting/pot roasting/poaching and braising). Saw off any protruding bone ends and remove any surplus fat. Pad bones with foil. Do not stuff boned and rolled joints. Wrap individual joints in cling film or foil, then overwrap in polythene bags. Exclude as much air as possible. Seal, label and freeze.

CHOPS, CUTLETS, ESCALOPES AND MEDALLIONS (for grilling/ frying/sautéeing/braising): Trim any bone ends and surplus fat. Beat out escalopes until very thin. Ideally do not cut more than 2.5 cm/1 inch thick. Pad any protruding bones with foil. Wrap individually in cling film or foil and interleave. Pack together in polythene bags. Exclude as much air as possible. Seal, label and freeze.

SLICES AND CUBES (for braising/casseroling/pies/stewing): Trim off surplus fat, sinews and gristle. Cut into 2.5 cm/1 inch thick slices or cubes if not already done. Pack in usable quantities in polythene bags. Exclude as much air as possible. Seal, label and freeze.

MINCED VEAL: Only freeze lean minced veal. Leave loose or shape into patties etc. Pack loose minced veal in usable quantities in polythene bags. Exclude as much air as possible. Seal, label and freeze.

STORAGE TIME: Joints for up to 12 months; chops, cutlets, escalopes and medallions for up to 12 months; slices and cubes for up to 3 months; and minced veal for up to 3 months.

TO DEFROST AND SERVE

JOINTS: Defrost in the wrappings at room temperature for 6-8 hours per kg/3-4 hours per lb, then cook as for fresh. Small boned and rolled joints under 1.5 kg/3 lbs and all joints on the bone can be cooked from frozen for approximately twice the usual cooking time until 77°C/170°F is registered on a meat thermometer. Do not cook boned and rolled joints from frozen.

CHOPS, CUTLETS, ESCALOPES AND MEDALLIONS: Thaw chops and cutlets in their wrappings at room temperature for 2-3 hours or in the refrigerator overnight, then cook as for fresh. Escalopes and medallions can be sautéed quickly in butter from frozen.

SLICES AND CUBES: Thaw in their wrappings at room temperature until the pieces separate, then cook as for fresh, allowing a little extra time and using the thawed juices.

MINCED VEAL: Partially defrost loose mince in its wrappings in the refrigerator, then cook as for fresh, stirring well to prevent sticking. Cook burgers, meatballs and patties from frozen.

USES: Veal can be cooked by many methods including roasting, pot roasting, braising, frying, grilling, casseroling, barbecuing and stewing.

VENISON

Venison, the flesh of the deer (usually red deer, roebuck and fallow deer) is generally considered as game. A haunch of venison consists of the loin and the leg whilst the forequarter is the shoulder and the best end of neck.

Venison generally needs to be hung for about 1 week before preparing for the freezer. Preparation of the carcass is similar to beef and all instructions relating to freezing are the same as beef. The storage time is up to 12 months. Venison is in season from June to January.

For freezing follow the instructions for freezing BEEF (page 38).

VOL-AU-VENTS

Vol-au-vents, perfect for filling for party time fare, can be frozen cooked or uncooked in the freezer with a good deal of success.

PREPARATION AND TO FREEZE

Prepare unbaked vol-au-vents in quantity for the freezer. Open freeze on trays until solid then pack in polythene bags, rigid boxes or foil. Seal, label and freeze.

Vol-au-vent cases can also be frozen baked but they are very fragile so should be placed in a rigid box. Seal, label and freeze.

STORAGE TIME: Up to 6 months.

TO DEFROST AND SERVE: Place frozen uncooked vol-au-vent cases on a baking sheet and cook from frozen in a very hot oven, 230°C/450°F/ Gas 8, for 15 minutes.

Leave baked vol-au-vent cases to defrost at room temperature for 1 hour or place frozen baked cases uncovered in a very hot oven, 230°C/450°F/Gas 8, for 5-10 minutes. Allow to cool then fill as required with meat, fish, poultry and vegetable mixtures in a sauce.

WATERMELONS

Because of their extremely high water content, watermelons cannot be frozen satisfactorily.

WHITEBAIT

Whitebait are very young herrings or sprats only about 4 cm/1½ inches long. They are generally available from March to December.

SELECTING FOR FREEZING
Freeze only very fresh supplies - ideally within 24 hours of the catch.

PREPARATION FOR FREEZING
Wash well then dry with absorbent kitchen paper.

TO FREEZE
Open freeze whole on trays until solid, then transfer to polythene bags or a rigid box. Seal, label and return to the freezer.

STORAGE TIME: Up to 2 months.

TO DEFROST AND SERVE: There is no need to defrost. Deep fry in oil, after dusting in flour, from frozen.

USES: Delicious as a starter with lemon wedges and brown bread and butter.

WHITING

Whiting is a small cod-like fish usually only about 20-23 cm/8-9 inches long and weighing about 225 g/8 oz. It is usually sold whole or in fillets but deteriorates quickly so must only be frozen when very fresh. It is available all year round but at its best from December to February.

For freezing follow the instructions for freezing COD (see page 69).

WINE LEFTOVERS

SELECTING FOR FREEZING

As the freezing point of alcohol is lower than that of water, it is advisable to only freeze small quantities, eg wine left at the bottom of an opened bottle.

TO FREEZE

Freeze in ice cube trays and when solid transfer into polythene bags. Seal, label and freeze.

STORAGE TIME: Up to 6 months.

USES: Use in the preparation of casseroles, stews, gravies and sauces when required. Red wine cubes can be used when making punch or mulled wine, and white wine can be used to cool summer drinks or added to fresh fruit salad mixtures.

WOODCOCK

Also called wood grouse, this is a migratory bird, with a long beak like the snipe.

SELECTING FOR FREEZING

Woodcock are available in January and October but are at their best in November and December. Woodcock should be well hung but the skin should remain intact on plucking.

PREPARATION FOR FREEZING

If the woodcock is to be roasted then it is not usually drawn but if cooked by a different method then draw and wash thoroughly inside and out. Dry with absorbent kitchen paper and truss if necessary. Do not stuff and reserve the giblets separately, discarding the sac from the gizzard.

TO FREEZE

Pad protruding bones with foil, then wrap whole birds individually with foil and overwrap in polythene bags. If the game is very high then use several bags and seal each one tightly. Pack giblets in rigid containers, keeping livers separate for use in pâtés etc. Seal, label and freeze.

STORAGE TIME: Up to 6 months.

TO DEFROST AND SERVE: Woodcock must be thoroughly thawed before cooking and must be cooked immediately after defrosting. Thaw in the wrappings in the refrigerator for 12-15 hours, depending upon size. Thaw giblets in the container in the refrigerator for about 12 hours.

USES: One woodcock should be served per person. It is suitable for roasting, braising and grilling.

YEAST

Since yeast cells are destroyed by high temperatures, it is often supposed that freezing at low temperatures will also destroy them. Fortunately this is not so and many cooks may like to freeze fresh yeast (especially if they prefer it to the freeze-dried variety) since it is not always so readily available.

SELECTING FOR FREEZING
Buy from a reputable outlet like a good bakers and buy a quantity in a single block since it quickly loses its potency once broken.

PREPARATION FOR FREEZING
Cut into 15 g/½ oz or 25 g/1 oz cubes (the most typical quantities required in home baking recipes).

TO FREEZE
Wrap individually in freezer foil then place in a rigid container to store all together. Seal, label and freeze.

STORAGE TIME: Freeze for up to 12 months.

TO DEFROST FOR USE: Defrost in the wrapping, at room temperature, for about 30 minutes to use. To speed up the process, frozen yeast can be grated on a coarse grater and will be ready for use in about 10 minutes.

USES: To make bread doughs both sweet and savoury, pizza bases and yeasted pastries like Danish pastries and croissants.

YOGURTS

Commercially prepared yogurts contain a stabiliser which makes it possible to freeze them as below. It is not possible to imitate this domestically and home-made yogurt separates on defrosting.

SELECTING FOR FREEZING

Fruit and flavoured yogurts (such as chocolate and honey) and natural yogurt can be frozen, but always freeze only really fresh yogurts.

PREPARATION FOR FREEZING

5 ml/1 teaspoon of sugar can be stirred into one small carton of natural unsweetened yogurt to stop any tendency to separate when defrosted. Sweetened natural, fruit and flavoured yogurts freeze successfully without adding extra sugar.

TO FREEZE

Yogurts can be frozen in their retail cartons but be sure they are well sealed. Seal, label and freeze.

STORAGE TIME: Up to 1 month.

TO DEFROST AND SERVE: Defrost overnight in the refrigerator for best results but they can be thawed more quickly at room temperature if needed in a hurry.

USES: As a breakfast and dessert dish, in cheesecakes, mousses, whips, gelatine-based puddings and for making raitas for curries.

INDEX

pâtés 125
pawpaws 119
peaches 126
pears 126
peas 125-6
peppers 127
persimmons 127-8
pet foods 128
pheasants 128-9
pies 123,124
    meat 111
pigeons 129
pineapples 129-30
pizzas 130
plaice 131
plums 131-2
polythene bags 18-19
pomegranates 132
pork 132-4
potatoes 134-5
    chips 66
poultry 28
    giblets 87-8
poussins 63
power cuts 12, 13
prawns 135-6, 149
puddings 154-5
puff pastry 123
pumpkins 136-7
purple sprouting
    broccoli 54-5

quails 137
quiches 137

rabbits 137-8
radishes
    summer 138
    winter 138-9
raspberries 139-40
ratatouille 140-1
re-freezing 26-7
record books 19-20
red cabbage 51-2
red mullet 141
redcurrants 76-7
refrigerator/

freezer 8, 11
rhubarb 142-3
rice 141-2
rock salmon 143
runner beans 143-4

saithe 70
salads 144
salmon 144-5
salmon trout 145
salsify 146
sandwiches 146-7
    toasted 161
satsumas 147
sauces 28, 147-8
sausagemeat 149
sausages 148-9
scallops 149
scampi 149
scones 150
scorzonera 146
seakale beet 159
sealing 24
self-seal bags 20
shortbread 41-2
shortcrust pastry 123
shrimps 150
skate 150
smoked haddock 151
snipe 151
sole 151-2
sorbets 152
soufflés 152
soups 28, 153
spinach 153-4
spinach beet 159
sponge cakes 53
sponge flans 85-6
sponge puddings
    154-5
sprats 154
spring cabbage 52-3
sprouts 48-9
squab 154
steamed puddings
    154-5
stews 28, 57

stick beans 143-4
stock 155
storage times 26
strawberries 155-6
stuffings 156
suet 156
suet pastry 124-5
suet puddings 157
swede 157
sweetcorn 158
swiss chard 159
swiss rolls 53
syrup packs 24-5

tangerines 160
tartlet cases 123, 124
tarts 160
teabreads 160-1
temperatures 23, 25
thermometers
    freezer 11
    meat 18
tomatoes 161-2
trout 163
turbot 163
turkey 164-5
turnips 166

ugli fruit 166-7
upright freezers 7-8, 11

veal 167-9
vegetables 27-8
venison 169
vol-au-vents 169

watermelons 170
waxed cartons and
    board 20
whipping cream 74
white cabbage 51-2
whitebait 170
whitecurrants 76-7
whiting 170
wine 171
woodcock 171-2

yeast 172
yogurts 173